"The greatest leaders I know lead by example. They are role models who adhere to standards they set for others and never ask more of them than they demand of themselves. Great leaders don't just 'manage' or 'motivate.' They inspire courage, tenacity, perseverance, resilience, and commitment in all who work with them. Greg Stube is such a leader—and an American hero.

"In Conquer Anything, *Greg draws on a lifetime of 'lessons learned' as a highly decorated U.S. Army Special Forces medic in this lucid, straightforward resource for parents, teachers, students, athletes, employers, supervisors, and soldiers. If 'success' is in your vocabulary,* Conquer Anything *is a must read."*

—Oliver L. North, Lt. Col USMC (Ret.), host of *War Stories* on FOX News

"Greg Stube's book, Conquer Anything, *shows us through his harrowing story how to stand up for freedom to become embodiments of the American dream. This is more than a Special Forces book, this is a guide to creating our own A-Teams to help us succeed in life and business."*

—Chris Cox, executive director of the NRA Institute for Legislative Action

"This is the best translation of how to effectively translate and use the United States Military Special Operations ethos in your everyday work environment. Great military stories combined with life lessons learned, bring this book from the battlefield to the boardroom. A great read!"

—Scott McEwen, #1 *New York Times* coauthor of *American Sniper, American Commander,* and the bestselling *Sniper Elite* series of novels

"My friend Greg Stube provides a defining example of an American who has met the call to duty as a human being, a father, a heroic combat disabled Green Beret, a life coach for vulnerable children, and a motivational speaker for corporate leaders and the FBI. Conquer Anything: A Green Beret's Guide to Building Your A-Team *is an exceptional roadmap to success for individuals, families, corporations, and government entities. Greg has distilled hard-won lessons from his extraordinary life experiences to illuminate how each person can create the future they want."*

—Chuck Deleot, Captain US Navy (Ret.), president of the Patriot Foundation

CONQUER ANYTHING

FOREWORD BY LT. GENERAL JOHN F. MULHOLLAND

CONQUER ANYTHING

A GREEN BERET'S GUIDE TO BUILDING YOUR A-TEAM

GREG STUBE

A POST HILL PRESS BOOK

Conquer Anything:
A Green Beret's Guide to Building Your A-Team
© 2018 by Greg Stube
All Rights Reserved

ISBN: 978-1-68261-483-9
ISBN (eBook): 978-1-68261-484-6

Cover art by Christian Bentulan
Interior Design and Composition by Greg Johnson, Textbook Perfect

Post Hill Press
New York • Nashville
posthillpress.com

Published in the United States of America

*I chose for this book to be released in May because
I want to dedicate it to the real fabric of America,
to every mother back in Fort Living Room
who is behind every man and woman who served
or is serving this great nation.*

CONTENTS

FOREWORD

Three hours after being dropped off at our insertion point, our rifle platoon had moved less than one hundred meters into the Panamanian jungle on a crushingly hot, humid, tropical afternoon in August 1979. The portion of the jungle where we were to enter must have been severely cut back some years ago, and now the jungle had returned with a vengeance. Towering well above our heads, the seemingly endless wall of elephant grass, massive vines thick with thorns, young black palm trees wrapped in their leather-piercing needles, and every other kind of vegetation imaginable actively resisted all our efforts to cut, hack, or slither our way through it. All the while, every kind of ant, hornet, and nasty stinging thing attacked us in their endless numbers. That, combined with the vegetation, created the most hostile, unyielding physical environment young Second Lieutenant John Mulholland had ever experienced.

I had been assigned as a platoon leader of an infantry platoon within an infantry battalion in the old Panama Canal Zone a mere seven days earlier. That day had begun with my introductory office call with our battalion commander. He was a very distinguished combat veteran with multiple combat tours in Vietnam, and the kind of man and officer whose presence alone commanded respect. To be honest, reporting to him was pretty intimidating to this young lieutenant fresh from the Infantry Officer Basic Course at Fort Benning, Georgia. At the end of our interview, his last words to me, I now realize, were really the beginning of my leadership experience as an officer in our Army. He literally fixed me in place with the stern gaze that he was well known for and said, "I'm assigning you to Third Platoon, Charlie Company... the worst platoon in the battalion."

Now the soldiers and non-commissioned officers of that platoon were staring at their new "LT" (slang for a lieutenant) with something significantly less than love and enthusiasm in their eyes. We were already hours behind schedule and all the men were very tired from the hours of fighting the heat and humidity, the jungle, and the "flying teeth." Truth be told, the men had come to this training mission with a noticeable lack of enthusiasm. The fact that their platoon was given the most undesirable of all the training areas for this five-day exercise, Panama's notorious Mohinga Swamp, as a consequence of their platoon leader being "the new guy," only added to their already low motivation. But, now, it was clearly decision time. We had to do something. I was getting no help, no recommendations from my NCOs (non-commissioned officers). They, too, were looking for a way out. Their faces told me everything I needed to know—this decision was all on me. Welcome to leadership.

Although I don't believe most of us find ourselves making decisions while baking beneath a tropical sun and being molested by evil, flying, biting things, I do believe it's common that many of us frequently find ourselves as the person "in the spotlight"—the accountable individual responsible for ensuring something gets done under difficult conditions. Sometimes that responsibility and accountability is specific and well articulated. Other times, it may be implied, and, in some cases, it might simply emerge as a result of circumstance. It may be at home, at work, or anywhere. Regardless, conditions manifest themselves that demand someone to step in, assess a situation, balance outcome and risk, and make a decision that he or she is willing to be held accountable for; in short, there is a need for a leader.

I had the honor and privilege of serving in the greatest army in the world, an army that places an absolute premium on leadership and its centrality to everything that happens, or fails to happen. In the course of my career, I have enjoyed the privilege of being trained and educated about leadership, to observe leadership in action, and to embrace the expectations the organization has of its leaders. That commitment to leadership began from the moment I enrolled in my university's Reserve Officer Training Corps program, and it has continued throughout my nearly 38-year career. But I also know that, outside of the military, specific and organizational focus, training, and continuing education on developing leaders is relatively rare. This is why I believe Sergeant 1st Class

FOREWORD

(Ret.) Greg Stube has made a powerful contribution to those seeking to be better leaders with this new book, *Conquer Anything, A Green Beret's Guide to Building Your A-Team.*

Greg is a medically retired Army Special Forces veteran of twenty-three years service to our country, most of that time spent as a Special Forces Medical Sergeant. The men of the U.S. Army Special Forces, commonly referred to as "the Green Berets," specialize in the art and practice of what we call "unconventional warfare." This mission specialty requires Special Forces teams to be prepared to live and operate alongside indigenous populations suffering under the yoke of oppression or occupation. Each Green Beret must devote himself to enduring focus and training, not only on the operational skill sets each Special Forces Soldier has, such as medical sergeant, weapons sergeant, and engineer sergeant, to name a few, but also on critical skills such as foreign language proficiency and studies in specific cultural understanding. While conducting combat operations with his operational detachment against the Taliban in Afghanistan, Greg was grievously wounded—wounds that very nearly killed him.

Not only did Greg fight back and win the most difficult fight of his life, the fight to live, but he also took that experience to heart and has since become a motivational speaker and trainer, sharing his experiences and advice with Americans across this great country. Part of his life's new mission is to share what he's absorbed, learned, and used about leadership as an Army Special Forces' professional through his new book about leadership.

Greg wrote this book to appeal to the broadest possible audience. Anyone can benefit from the advice, recommendations, and insights from the personal examples Greg uses throughout the book to more deeply understand what it means to be a leader. Greg stresses the value of applying a consistent framework to one's leadership challenges, whether they are simple or complex. Most importantly, he brings to the forefront the critical linkage of character, ethics, humility, and integrity which are essential components of a good leader's decision-making foundation.

Over thirty-seven years of service in the U.S. Army, with over thirty-four of that in Army Special Forces, has left me with the unshakeable belief that leadership is the cornerstone of every undertaking that takes place within the sphere of human interaction. If leadership is important to you, read *Conquer Anything.* You will be a significantly better leader for it.

—*Lt. General John F. Mulholland, U.S. Army, Retired*

INTRODUCTION

We Kept Running Out of Ammo

"Everybody has a plan 'til they get hit in the mouth."

—MIKE TYSON

A bullet smashed into my side of the steel chicken plate in the turret on the top of the Humvee and ricocheted away. I ducked deeper into the Humvee's gun turret and glanced back across the red ground to an adobe wall 50 meters away. Someone was back there. Someone who was trying to kill me with an AK-47 was on that wall.

I couldn't turn the whole gun turret around to face the Taliban fighter as bullets were banging into the front of the steel plate in twos and threes. All I could do was rely on my team to take care of the fighter before he got me or someone else.

Our column of twenty vehicles—a dozen Humvees and eight light trucks being used by Afghanistan National Army (ANA) soldiers—were filled with twenty-nine other Green Berets and about fifty ANA soldiers. We had run into an ambush. Machineguns were pounding at us and brass was falling hot onto the red earth as we returned fire.

In those tense seconds, I could feel my back itching as if I were expecting a bullet. I was wielding death and waiting for death, but I wasn't waiting complacently. I don't recall what I said into my "whisper mic," a headset connected to the team of Green Berets around me. I like to think what I said was controlled, calm. I'd been in the Army eighteen years, by then, fourteen of them with the Green Berets. So, dammit, I was no cherry, but, in the frantic blur of this desperate moment amid days and nights of gunfights in those rough hills far from base, I don't recall precisely what I said or how I said it.

INTRODUCTION

I do remember looking behind me and clearly seeing branch clippings falling as that Taliban fighter fired bursts from his AK-47 from the top of an adobe wall and through some brush. I remember seeing that brush disintegrate in slow motion, and can still see in my mind's eye what the clippings from the branches looked like as they fell. You don't, of course, see the detailed pieces as they fall, but you see the blur, the movement, the displacement, and the blast, and your mind fills in the rest.

I also remember when the second and third bullets smashed into my side of the chicken plate. I was on the whisper mic, asking someone—anyone—to kill the Taliban fighter before he got me or someone else.

For that crazy moment, I felt alone, naked. Still, I kept firing bursts of .50-caliber ammo into Taliban positions in front of the red rocks and to the sides along the adobe walls in the late-afternoon desert light. As I did, I contemplated feelings of mortality for fleeting moments as I had several times before. In moments of true fear, what even a Special Forces' guy wants can be the same as anyone else. At times like this, what we want is our mommy, or warmth and safety of any kind. But that's not there, so you are left with a feeling of mental solitude, as if you are hunkered down within yourself and searching fast for solutions. After that moment ran through me like a cold shiver, I felt the team more acutely alive around me and with me than ever before, as if the twenty-nine other Green Berets were a part of me.

SFC Sean Mishra, who was driving the Humvee, had screamed, "Grenade!"

Sean, another Special Forces' soldier, had leapt out of the vehicle to get the nearby Taliban fighter. At that time, Sean was a trainer for ANA soldiers. He was a big, quiet, strong, and tall hombre. He was the best driver I'd ever seen, and I felt like he would be the best at anything he did. He was one of those guys who are always calm in a storm. He had taken on a "Big John" persona for many of us, like the Jimmy Dean song about a giant of a man who performed heroically to save others. He just couldn't sit there behind the wheel, waiting for me to get it in the back.

This was the fourth day of our mission moving deep into the belly of Taliban country south and west of Kandahar to cut off the escape routes of the Taliban fighters as Canadian and ANA soldiers moved in from the north. We could see our objective by this time, a sort of pyramid-shaped hill known as Sperwan Ghar that was maybe a kilometer in front of us.

We'd kicked a hornet's nest of Taliban fighters as we closed in on what intelligence told us was the very place where the Taliban movement had been born. We had contact from three directions. Well, that's dry, military talk. What I mean is machineguns and RPGs (rocket-propelled grenades) were being shot at us by who knows how many Taliban fighters from three directions.

Sean had screamed "grenade" after he'd leapt out of the vehicle and tried to throw a grenade at the enemy position. His intention was to throw it over the adobe wall that the Taliban fighter was using for cover, but the grenade didn't clear the wall. Sean had served quite a bit of active duty by then. He also trained Afghans, but, like many of us, he had obviously never rehearsed throwing a grenade when wearing full-body armor. As his arm came forward, it ran into his chest plate, causing his arm to stop and the grenade to fall within twenty feet of our Humvee. He kicked sand to run to the other side of our vehicle where he was exposed to even more enemy fire and hit the ground.

I dropped down into the vehicle. Moments later, the grenade exploded, rocking the Humvee. I stood up again into the gun turret and saw shrapnel marks near the bullet dings on my side of the chicken plate.

Sean was apologizing, asking if I was okay. I could hear his voice on the headset in my helmet. When I said, "Yes," Sean said he was about to throw another grenade. I watched this grenade make a beautiful arc toward the adobe wall, but then bounce off the top of the wall and come rolling back our way. We had to take cover all over again, and this grenade boomed. Meanwhile, machine gun fire and RPGs were still coming from three directions, and the enemy behind me was still alive and shooting.

Other Green Berets around us had heard our conversation over the whisper mics. SSG Zack Harrison, a former school teacher and coach that 9/11 had turned into a real-life Chuck Norris, saw what was happening, turned, and leveled an MK-19 grenade launcher (also known as the Mark 19), a 40 mm belt-fed automatic grenade launcher that was first developed during the Vietnam War, at that section of adobe wall behind us. He sprayed the wall and the area beyond it with grenades. The Taliban fighter who had almost had me was blown into bone fragments.

Zack was tougher than woodpecker lips and had a mission focus, matched with a level of competence, that no enemy could prepare for. I didn't even pause to thank him. I don't even think Zack knew what a difference he made as he moved on to the next target as he was just doing his job. No time for that in battle. I just got back on the .50-caliber machine gun and felt it *boom-boom-boom* out ammo, saw the bullet splashes on rocks and adobe walls, and saw Taliban fighters pop up as they tried to advance and then smashed down by .50-caliber bullets.

Then a command came over our headsets calling for an organized retreat. Basically, what happens is everyone fires whatever they've got left all at once at a high rate in the direction of the enemy. We'll do this for maybe thirty seconds as the drivers get the vehicles ready to leave all at once. Then, on command, everyone stops shooting and the drivers race us away. By the time the enemy realizes we're driving away, we're out of their effective kill range.

We timed this to coincide with an incoming airstrike. Air support is in constant communication with us as they come in. They tell us when they are a minute from hitting their targets, and then, typically, again at thirty seconds.

As we drove away fast, those Taliban, seeing us retreating, got brave and jumped out of cover as they fired on us. This exposed them to the incoming ordinance they didn't know was coming down on them. I saw the plumes of brown dust rising as the bombs hit the enemy positions. Now *that's* teamwork. In everyday life, this would be horrifying stuff, but in our desensitized state, it only evoked deep sighs of relief and even ear-to-ear grins. This with the knowledge we'd have that many fewer to fight alone.

So, yeah, we were retreating from hundreds of Taliban fighters, but we weren't giving up. We fell back about three kilometers to a wide open, flat area in that arid wasteland between oases of marijuana fields with plants much taller than me and villages that looked almost Stone Age. We knew trying to hide all our vehicles would be foolhardy. Our night-vision capability and weapons, which gave us much better range than the Taliban fighters, would keep us safer in the open at night than trying to hide in the terrain. We weren't allowed to use our night-vision advantages in offensive operations at that time because the Afghanistan National Army (ANA) with us didn't have the training or equipment to hunt Taliban at night. However, we did harness our night vision's full defensive potential by scanning for approaching fighters.

We circled the vehicles and set up a perimeter. Our total force included three A-Teams of Green Berets—thirty soldiers in all—and about fifty

ANA soldiers. I found that none of our men were badly wounded as I did my rounds as the senior medic.

We did have to medevac out one ANA soldier. He had accidentally shot himself in the hand. This happens so often it's unbelievable. The ANA soldiers like to stand with a gun's barrel resting on their foot and with one hand holding the butt of the rifle, or the barrel up with a hand or wrist covering the muzzle as they use their other hand to smoke. All too often somehow—maybe because the rifle slips and they use their cigarette hand to grab it and stupidly jerk the trigger—one of them shoots a hole in his own hand or foot. I have never witnessed how the negligent discharges actually take place, but I've always wondered what kind of circus act it takes to depress the trigger in that way. It's worth the time we put into our training to avoid minor distractions like shooting your own hand off.

Our leadership spent two hours that night going over the maps and calling in questions to command as they made plans. They then called us together to let us know what the plan was. I have always enjoyed listening to leaders contemplate what is being faced in grave situations. I liked this part of the process because it directly affected me, and because seeing human nature tested in those ways is deep stuff. There are no second chances. A leader has to do everything they can to make the right decision the first time. A good team with open communication up the chain of command is so important. It's life and death on a Special Forces team at these moments. As a result, my respect for leaders and team players is undying.

Yup, we were going back in after sunrise. We took this news solemnly, but deep in our thoughts was the general conviction that we'd have preferred to go in at night. We *owned* the night. We had night-vision capabilities. The enemy didn't. We'd trained a lot at night for these missions. We could have hunted Taliban at night like the alien did by day in the movie *Predator*. But the credit for the victory was to go to the ANA soldiers, and they didn't know how to fight at night, so we had to take even bigger risks and give up our tactical advantage to fight the Taliban in daylight. Constraints and restraints are a part of life, but they can degrade the morale of a team. Resentment from these constraints can break a team's dynamic and stall its momentum, and we were doing all we could not to let this happen by not talking about it.

We set up infrared beacons, little flashing lights we call "fireflies," a minimum of 300 meters from our location in order for the C-130s to drop us pallets of munitions and other supplies. These come down without flares and are as quiet as a light wind rattling sheets on a clothesline. You can sometimes glimpse these pallets falling fast under parachutes against the stars. They fall swiftly and hit the ground with a roar. If a pilot misses his drop point and one lands on you, you'll never know it—some letter home, and that's it.

The night was eerie. We slept, if we could, in shifts. Between naps, we'd sit behind thermal scopes, watching for the enemy. Conversations were whispered and short. No one bitched or talked about dying. That doesn't happen in an A-Team in this type of situation. There might be a few private conversations between two close men about their wives or girlfriends back stateside, but none of that is made public. Special Forces, at such times, are not robots, but they have been trained to be a team. Anything that detracts from the mission is controlled or even eliminated.

During that dark night, under a bright sea of stars twinkling with no light pollution to dim them, we weren't thirty separate men. We were *one* team. We also weren't thirty men all cut from the same cloth or molded into the same war machine. We had common values and had gone through much of the same intense training, but we all had different personalities and specialties within the team. Like a football team with its quarterback, linebackers, and so on, our team members had to fill many roles to make the team into a fighting unit.

Any team, especially an A-Team, can't be a monolithic thing. These teams are dynamic fighting machines because they are many parts that fit together. In a regular Army unit, orders are given and basically applied, but not questioned. There is a brain and a body. But Green Berets are all trained to be parts of the brain *and* body. Anyone can quickly bring in new information and he or she is trained to share it quickly and effectively. In fact, the Special Forces have the distinctive practice of having the members of the team combine their subject matter expertise to construct their own plan as a team. This is unheard of elsewhere in the military, where plans are handed down for execution. Once the plan is completed, command is briefed and the mission is either approved or we are asked to rethink something. When we do have a plan, the team responds together. The members of an A-Team know one another like we know our right and left arms. Moving together, thinking together, becomes natural.

So when the pallets of ammo hit the ground, they were quickly broken down and distributed among the Humvees. These were organized so we could reload them quickly when the next day's gunfight began. Little of this had to be discussed. We all knew what our parts were. We were receivers running perfect routes and blockers forming an impenetrable wall. We even kept a running count of ammo and supplies, so we knew who needed more and who needed less. Without training and rehearsing, this would never have worked this smoothly.

Looking back at this now, I know that team leadership in our lives, our families, our businesses, and in our armed forces comes down to the same principles, but I also see that to achieve our dreams, we must dispel some big misunderstandings. The best way to explain this isn't to preach, but to show you, which is why I began with this true story at such a dramatic point. Things were about to get hot, really hot, and it was the team that made us formidable—the weapons, equipment, and technology were just the tools the team used.

But, now, to really show you how an A-Team works so you can apply their skills to your life, we need to step back a few days to when I made this big, bold decision I don't regret even though it resulted in my body and life being blown apart. I want to tell you all about this clearly, honestly, and humbly because it's not about me, but about giving back to America all that this struggle has given me. I owe you these lessons learned on the battlefield in the service of our country.

PART ONE
THE "I" IN TEAM

"We few, we happy few, we band of brothers;
For he today that sheds his blood with me
Shall be my brother; be he ne'er so vile,
This day shall gentle his condition."

—WILLIAM SHAKESPEARE, *KING HENRY V*, ACT 4, SCENE 3

1

THE DECISION

All Great Leaders Begin with This Conscious Choice

"Purpose affirms trust, trust affirms purpose, and together they forge individuals into a working team."

—GENERAL STANLEY McCHRYSTAL

The red earth under my striding feet had been stomped hard by a thousand combat boot heels. The sun was hot over Kandahar, and the base was busy between the HESCO barriers (collapsible wire-mesh containers filled with dirt and rocks), sandbags, concertina wire, and concrete perimeters. It was late August 2006, and I was going to volunteer for Operation Medusa, a mission every American should know about, but few do. I saw a patrol coming in through the gates and paused to watch the sand-colored Humvees and the men in their battle gear, desert camouflage, and dusty goggles, and I knew I'd soon be out there with them again. I turned on my heel and kept going.

I see this scene now in my mind like it's some clichéd part in a Hollywood war movie. Not that I'm casting myself as some kind of hero. No, we'll get to all that. I see it that way because I was so simplistic then, and because I now understand the strengths and weaknesses of the well-defined part I was playing as I entered that A-Team of Green Berets about to go on a mission that would be a key part of the biggest single battle of the war. I was like an actor who immerses himself in a character, only I wasn't aware I was doing this. I was completely in step with the Green Beret ideal. I was a badass Special Forces soldier fighting for good, and I let that warrior persona define me, even put blinders on me.

Playing a role is important in anything we do in life. The key is to know we are playing a part so that we don't become two-dimensional in our thinking. This is important because, though there are many quarterbacks, only a few leaders have the right personality and enough experience to decompress a stressful situation as it unfolds. To the rest of us, we seem to have no time to react. But the ideal quarterback is able to act in decisive and timely ways within spaces that leave the rest of us struggling to catch up with what just happened. They can do this because they don't let outside worries, desires, and more get in their way. This is why playing a role is important—it allows us to have clarity of mind so we can do the right—even the impossible—thing in the stress of an important moment.

In the same way, they are able to see early on how the little things add up to what we all see in the big picture—to a successful outcome. I was good at playing my part and contributing, but maybe a bit of a late bloomer in getting the bigger picture in relation to my actions and identity at the time. Now I describe it as maturity, but this is something I wouldn't have admitted to then.

So, yeah, I thought I knew myself at that time. I was one of the toughest men on the planet, and I fought for peace, for freedom. We define ourselves by our enemies, and we had a stark contrast to compare ourselves with. We were fighting an enemy who'd sheltered Osama bin Laden, an enemy who denigrates women, who defaces others' beliefs, who murders innocents, who suppresses human individuality, who wants to turn us all back to the Dark Ages while claiming all of this is God's will. There was no confusion in my mind, not then. I knew exactly who I was and what I was fighting for.

Funny, though, how I'd laugh then at the cartoonish parodies Hollywood often passes off for Special Forces soldiers. I'd think, *That's not us. That's some* GI Joe *cartoon character*. Then I'd toss my head and think, if those screenwriters and directors only knew what Green Berets really are like and what we do, well, *then* they could tell some stories about A-Teams. Oh, boy, they could tell stories that would make you jump up and start belting out "God Bless America." They could tell some stories that mean something, that would make your skin go all goose bumps, that could even help people understand when we must fight and when we shouldn't. They could even show where the military goes dead wrong—which isn't at all where they think it is. All that would take honesty in the most extreme sense, and Hollywood is rarely into that these days.

But, the truth is, there was a lot I didn't get then, either. Arrogance has a way of blinding you, especially when you've seen so much, when you've seen things all those people back home don't know anything about, not really. You know this, and it makes you conceited. Yes, I've seen the enemy, and he is me.

So when I look back at my Green Beret persona before Operation Medusa and all that would come after, I know how right I was about a lot of it, but how so very blind I was too. My strict adherence to what a Green Beret should be actually became a weakness. The complete devotion to this ideal is why so many of our returning soldiers are not recovering from Post-Traumatic Stress Disorders (PTSD). Perhaps much of our training leaves out the fact that we are human, and no matter how much we prepare, we can never escape the cascades of feelings and emotions that inevitably rush in. Again, this is why we must understand the roles we play. Technical and tactical proficiency just aren't enough to overcome the fact that our own hearts and minds go with us into these dark places to do unthinkable things.

But now I wonder if I can show you this shattering of my Green Beret perspective without making you think I'm condemning everything I stood for. So I'll first say this straight out: Just because I had to die on the operating table and miraculously come back and struggle through a darkness in which many get lost before seeing how wrong I was about myself and so much else doesn't mean what I stood for was wrong. It was just that I was only half of what we all should be. I'll get deeper into that later, but, right now, I'll just say it takes a hell of a lot of truth to live right. I found out that much.

So, as I walked in to volunteer for Operation Medusa, there were soldiers rushing here and there in the August sun on errands related to war. The base had the officious feel and layout those temporary military installations do—spend time in one such base and you'll know where the mess hall, the latrines, and the barracks all must be. Not far away, I knew there were young men leaning over machine guns, peering across this sea of red earth into the moving mirages of heat waves outside Kandahar, all hoping to see the Taliban coming. This viewpoint might sound fatalistic to some, but young soldiers almost universally long to be tested by fire, even if few of them know a damn thing about all that.

I had been tested, and so I should have had my perspective blown open already. By then, I'd been a Green Beret for fourteen of the eighteen years I'd been in the U.S. Army. I was thirty-seven years old. I had no doubt I was a veteran of the toughest breed alive. I lived by the creed of an iconic warrior. I'd learned over years of training and missions to live up to this ideal. This Green Beret part is consuming; when a Green Beret is at his best, he personifies this ideal. All through our years of training, our struggle was to be this perfect soldier Hollywood portrays but barely comprehends. This Green Beret ideal is at first presented as a perfect possibility. For those few who pass the gauntlets of tests, both physical and mental, this ideal grows into a possession.

I was pumped up when I reached the plywood front door to a building constructed from cement blocks on that base outside Kandahar, as it was the literal entrance to what I'd spent my life training for. The building had ponchos strung over its windows, and when I pulled open its front door, I found another poncho hung to hide the scene inside when the door was opened.

I did pause then, just for a moment, and remembered what I'd promised my family back home: I wouldn't "volunteer for anything stupid." But, dammit, I was a Green Beret. They'd understand. I'd taught men to be Green Berets at the U.S. Army John F. Kennedy Special Warfare Center and School (SWCS)—known informally as "SWC"—at Fort Bragg for four years. I was an instructor at SWC on September 11, 2001. I had to stay there for years after that horrific day. Imagine that, spending years training Green Berets to fight battles you'd been trained for yourself. You go home to your soft life and play with your son and feel like you're some kind of poser, a man who teaches but doesn't do.

After 9/11, I was even one of the Special Forces' instructors tasked with creating a program designed to expedite the creation of Green

Berets ready for the battlefield. At the time, Special Forces guys with years in the Green Berets like I had called the graduates of this expedited program "SF Babies," though I've now lost the taste for that elitist and false phrase.

I was at SWC too many times when news came back that someone I'd trained was coming home in a body bag. Some of those men were killed on their first mission. These were fine men who'd struggled and endured and earned a place among the elite. They were the best America can produce. Many of them had given up professional sports careers, medical practices, lucrative businesses, and more, to answer the call and dedicate all they were to the cause. But if they were going to do this, they wanted to be the best. I had seen enough of the hot zones of the world to know that many of those who die in war did everything they were trained to do, but still a bullet or a bomb found them. I knew this and more, but I was still frustrated that I wasn't in the fight.

Like all Green Berets, I went through Airborne (parachute) Training at Fort Benning, Georgia. I got my wings and went through the Special Forces Assessment and Selection course and then the Special Forces Qualification course. I then spent about 57 weeks at the Special Forces Qualification course at Fort Bragg, North Carolina, before going to Phase 3 of the Special Forces Qualification course. After that, I spent six months learning Russian at the Special Forces Language School at Fort Bragg.

All that was just the preliminary training to see if I was good enough to be a Green Beret. Next came more specialized training. If I failed any of those stages, I'd have been reassigned to regular Army infantry. The Special Forces training pipeline has a washout rate so high the Army would rather not publish that statistic. I was one of the few to make it through. Sure, you have to be smart and tough to pass all that, but you also have to be lucky. I saw good men go down because they rolled an ankle in jump school or pulled a muscle during a navigation course in the very grueling mental and physical process of trying to be a member of the Special Forces. Mr. Murphy was always there to threaten the dreams of great soldiers. Many times, I somehow slipped through the cracks in testing as I watched someone better than I am have a bad day and go home to make other plans.

Through this training, you are a soldier—in my case, a Special Forces' soldier. Your uniform has creases in the right places. Your beret is cocked on your head at just the right angle to show honor, pride, and bravado. You are doing everything to live up to the ideal of what a Green Beret is supposed to be. You can get lost in this ideal. He is like your perfect self, and you want to be him. You shut off other thoughts and desires. You pare away anything that contradicts this ideal. You live that way, *really* live that way, and the Army loves you for this. They see this in you. They trust you because you are in step with their ideal. This isn't a bad thing; it's a very useful thing. An A-Team like this can do things others can't.

Now, I'm not saying Green Berets become some sort of machines. Green Berets aren't like Army infantry. Green Berets are taught to think and to lead. They aren't a mindless team blindly following orders. They are all a part of the "brain" helping the "body" (the unit or team) achieve its goal, which is how any great team must work. I think it's easier to be detached when someone else is giving the orders. But when you are also part of the brain, you can't blindly follow. You are responsible for yourself and everyone with you. Further, when you are seen wearing that distinctive headgear and a tab sewn on your shoulder that reads "Special Forces," you are expected to be the one in any venue who will save the day. Once you decide to parade around with the appearance of all the wonder and greatness of those who actually built the reputation attached to that distinction, you find that it becomes impossible to be the common man anymore. Leadership becomes synonymous with simply leaving your house. This adds to the intensity of being a Green Beret. It consumes you.

When this part ends, as any part in life must, you are left lost in a sea of people, as you have so suppressed your own individual identity that it doesn't even seem to exist anymore. You are like a professional athlete who suddenly finds himself retired. All his life he'd been a football or baseball star, and then, suddenly, he is a has-been, a man with no living identity. This is made even worse when an athlete is injured in his prime. One day he is the ideal, and then, suddenly, what is he?

Or, worse, he risks being defined by his injury. Who wants to live with that identity? This is even more extreme for a soldier stationed at a foreign base in a hostile land, as he must live that part every hour of every day. He can't go home and take off the uniform and love his wife and sleep soundly knowing the only thing that'll wake him will be an alarm clock. In war, he must always be in character. He must always live on the edge with fear in every heartbeat, prepared to meet the end of his time on earth. He must let himself fall away as he goes headlong into what he was trained to become.

Now, a person who has lived this way, who has tried with every part of himself to stay in step with this iconic part, obviously wants to follow this ideal into battle. That's understandable, right? This is a good thing when you really believe you are fighting for good.

I had actually made it to Afghanistan only days before to serve as a Special Forces medic attached to a civil-affairs team. So I was in a unit focused on improving the livelihood of the local populace in Afghanistan. But two of my former students saw me coming out of the mess hall and came running up to me in the morning sun. "Sergeant Stube. We have this mission—it could be a real humdinger—and we need another medic," they whispered to me urgently. Their excitement was infectious. They were about to do what they'd spent years training for and wanted me along. I wanted to go. I wanted to stand behind what I'd taught.

I said, "I'll see what I can do," but I meant, *I'll move the bureaucratic Army with the sheer force of my will to make this happen.*

Going meant getting permission from Civil Affairs, Special Forces Command, and others, and getting the A-Team (Operational Detachment Alpha) I'd be joining to let me in. A team of Green Berets is a unit more tightly woven than any sports team could hope to be, as soldiers know if they fail, they die. They know even if they do everything right, they still might die. This reality binds them together in blood, and in what I call service beyond sacrifice.

A Green Beret A-Team works as if each member is an extension of one body. Each has a critical part to play. They have to know the team's SOPs (Standard Operating Procedures) and each other's strengths and weaknesses. Each is trained to think and make decisions as a situation changes and to communicate this with their team. There is no filler in a Green Beret A-Team. Members practice together so they can move as one down the field of battle. And I hadn't done any of that with this A-Team.

Still, if I didn't try to go, I'd be a hypocrite, not the warrior I'd spent my life becoming. I'd trained for this and spent years getting others ready for this kind of mission. Saying no just wasn't an option. My whole self-identity was fashioned for this. I had made my decision.

So I pushed the poncho aside and stepped into a dim, cave-like room.

The scene inside would barely be believable in a movie. Eight Green Berets were staring at me with the expressions of hungry wolves before a hunt. They were sitting and standing among piles of ammunition, automatic weapons, and explosives. One was breaking down an M4A1 carbine to clean out Afghanistan sand. Another was counting grenades for the M4's grenade launcher. A few were loading rifle magazines with 5.56 ammo. But all of them stopped when bright sunlight shot in with me. They all stayed still as a photograph; most were giving me the stink eye. Two who had been my students at SWC nodded at me, but didn't say anything.

Captain Rusty Bradley strode across the room, stepped over piles of ammo, and pushed me back through the green poncho and out the plywood door and into the bright sunlight with his palm on my chest.

Rusty had a heavy brown beard and intense eyes. He is over six feet tall with the build of a linebacker. I'm five feet, nine inches, and, then, weighed 180 pounds. I was a distance runner and could outmarch or outrun almost anyone into the dirt. Rusty was a big, John Wayne wannabe. He did good work on the team, but was also in search of a reputation through the process. He would carry out orders perfectly, but then retell them as his own version, as though he were the commanding general.

Rusty stopped pushing when we were well outside. He always thought of himself as a John Wayne character—don't apologize, as it was a sign of weakness. He lived that ethos in a way that would seem like an overdone character in a movie, but, out there, with what we had to do, his persona put soldiers at ease, as he was a man who was what he seemed. He was a man who lived the part so completely you knew he would be there doing the right thing when you found yourself in the throes of battle.

Out in the hot sun, and out of sight of his team, he was alive in his role as a captain of a Green Beret A-Team. As he looked me in the eyes, his expression softened. He dropped his hand from my chest but stayed at less than arm's length as he said, "Sergeant, I understand you have a young son at home. Besides, this late in your career, this might not be the best mission to volunteer for. Are you sure you want to do this?"

Here I was a senior E7 with 18 years in the service—only four years outside the Special Forces—and with Rusty I felt like a private again. That feeling made me recall how I actually felt as a private. Back then, I'd low crawl naked through broken glass to get my commander a cold drink. There was no brown nosing, no sucking up. I just wanted to impress. I wanted to show them they had an asset in me.

I looked right back into his eyes and asked, "Do you have kids at home?"

"Yeah, I've got a daughter."

"Why are you going?"

He nodded and reached out his hand. I shook his hand. Rusty had been in the 82nd Airborne Division. He was now a Special Forces Detachment Commander, an A-Team Leader. I have absolute respect for A-Team Leaders. There is a critical officer-to-sergeant relationship. Officers take command of an A-Team, but cycle out after a few years into upper leadership or choose other fields outside of the Special Forces. Sergeants stay for as long as they are capable, or until they reach retirement age. I had opted to stay a sergeant. I wanted to stay on an A-Team. It was the activity and identity I wanted until the end. I wanted the mission, with my boots on the ground. The visions of younger men seldom include the high price that comes with the territory.

Rusty put his right hand on my shoulder and led me back inside. He kept his hand on my shoulder as he introduced me to each member of the team. Riley, a medic, was updating IV bags and catheters. Rush was in the middle of the room, checking weapons, all the belt-fed machine guns. Bill, a sergeant I'd taught at SWC, no longer had the inquisitive look of a student; he'd earned the salty demeanor of a warrior who'd already proven himself. Everyone else was carefully going over their gear.

I was an unknown to most of them. I hadn't been through mission prep with them. We only had about 36 hours before we'd go on a mission that would take us through the soft sand dunes of the Red Desert, through canyons with terrain that looked like ambush spots in classic Western movies, and then to villages filled with Taliban so we could block escape routes back to Pakistan and elsewhere that Taliban fighters might use when a large force of Canadian and Afghan National Army (ANA) soldiers moved in from the north. If I was going to fit in, I had a lot to do.

The predatory expressions of the other Green Berets softened. They were willing to give me a chance, but still weren't so sure about me. I was a very senior medic, and only a certain kind of dude will be a pecker checker for a living. Usually, a medic is a little off—they tend to be the oddball in the bunch. The character "Joker" (played by Mathew Modine) in Stanley Kubrick's 1987 flick *Full Metal Jacket* was the kind of guy who'd become a Green Beret medic. You need those kinds of guys around, when they're medics, anyway, but you don't necessarily want them too close. You definitely don't want them to feel they have to check on you—that means something is wrong.

After introducing me to the team, Rusty asked, "Greg, in a movement column, what do you see yourself doing?"

Medical Sergeants in the Green Berets, you see, aren't like traditional Army Medics. A Green Beret medic has all the same training as any other Green Beret; they just also have years of medical training in how to treat everything from a toothache to wounds from a .50-caliber machine gun. A Special Forces medic's primary training is trauma medicine, but they also have a working knowledge of surgery, anesthesia, orthopedics, pharmacology, minor dentistry, veterinary care, water quality, preventive medicine, and too much more to list. Special Forces Medical Sergeants are also often trained to be qualified combat divers, HALO parachutists, snipers, and more. They receive more than 60 weeks of formal classroom training and practice exercises. I had interned in hospital emergency rooms in New York City and other trauma care centers and hospitals where I worked 16-hour shifts treating gunshot wounds, stabbings, and everything else that came in the door. You don't want combat to be your first experience providing trauma care.

So I told Rusty to just put me in wherever he had a hole.

Rusty wasn't sure. Then Dave, a weapons sergeant from Ohio, asked, "Can you shoot a .50?"

I said, "I can set the headspace and timing on a .50-caliber machine gun in under 50 seconds. I've been shooting one since 1988." I wasn't boasting. The .50 was my baby. I had a lot of hours on those big machine guns.

He grinned. Now they needed me on their A-Team.

So I went to work. I had to check the .50-caliber machine gun I'd be manning at the top of a Humvee, I had to learn every facet of this mission, and I had to get my gear straight. Each Green Beret A-Team has its own SOPs, or Standard Operating Procedures. If you're wounded, others need to know right where your personal medical gear is, where your ammo is, and all of the rest of the 60 pounds you carry. The team needs to be able to function as one even in limited visibility.

As we went over the piles of gear, and as I learned every detail about the 10-day mission, I got to know the others on the team. This is another place where Hollywood doesn't have a clue. A team of Green Berets isn't boastful, and these men only get personal in private. If you strut around in a real Green Beret team while cracking stupid jokes, you'll get your ass kicked. There is no fooling around. This is real. Anyone not with the program won't make it. All these guys are badass alphas. Great humor is acceptable, but only with careful timing—and, often, this is dark humor that wouldn't be appropriate for the rest of society.

The culture is different than the regular Army. No one ever says, "Don't be a hero" to an A-Team. Regular Army infantry say, "Don't volunteer for nothin'." Those words are never spoken in the Special Forces, where everyone is doing everything they can. You'll never hear "That's not my job." On an A-Team, there is actually no verbal communication of those things. You are swimming with sharks, praying not to bleed. There is no discussion of feelings. You don't go into details on your personal life. The moment there is a crossroads where a conversation could go in an emotional direction, guys will get up and say, "Well, you did what had to be done." You could cut moments like that with a knife. This regimented self-control, this constant adherence to the ideal, gets so thick that such moments feel frigid. This can make it a sad, cold, and lonely way of living. Most of us come from childhoods, from family and friends, where we could get our feelings hurt by a comment. We might complain that one of our siblings was loved more or that something wasn't fair. Such things don't occur on a Green Beret A-Team. An A-Team is a cold and masculine space where it is not okay to be touched. Everything, even peoples' personal feelings, is controlled so we can completely focus on the mission.

But, sure, family is always open for discussion. It's a badge of honor to look out for your family. But you'd only mention them briefly, and maybe show a picture; you'd never talk about them in an emotional or meaningful way. There might be a one-on-one about a divorce or illness between two close Green Berets, but that would never be talked about in the open. If someone is killed, there is never a group boohoo session.

This carefulness with emotion, with personality, is especially relevant in a war zone. We're in this space far from home, and there are people in the hills who want to kill us. Out there, emotions can get you killed. They can make a man's mind wander at a critical moment, and they can lead to a breakdown where someone doesn't do the needed thing in a desperate moment.

Still, by God, you're out there with other human beings, and I couldn't help having recollections of school recess where someone wants to fight and you think, *Can't we talk about this?* I was 37 years old then, old enough to have perspective. I had a family. I had learned how to walk in different worlds. But, still, when you put on the uniform, it must be all business, so I shook my head free of such normal thoughts as much as that can be done. The Army had warmed up to the notion of family throughout my career, but I had been formed by a system that readily informed me that anything outside of what the Army had issued me wasn't of interest. Harsh, maybe, but it prepared me for the worst conditions that became reality.

When I saw my former students in the room—guys 15 years younger than I was—I was blown away that people I'd known as kids now had that steely-eyed look. They'd already passed the initial hurdle of anxiety. They were a team. This wasn't just a night patrol. These guys had been through life and death together.

And we were busy. We needed to pack the vehicles with as much ammo, fuel, munitions, and supplies as we could fit. But we tried not to inhibit our ability to move around inside the Humvees as we fought.

I recall a night mission that evening to abscond with cans of .50-caliber ammo from an aviation unit. We needed the larger ammo cans—in battle with a .50-caliber machine gun, the most dangerous time is when you're switching cans of ammo—and all we had were the smaller cans. We didn't have time to request them via the bureaucratic process that separates branches of the Armed Forces. So taking these ammo cans was good juvenile fun done with the precision of an A-Team. But when we got back, there was no backslapping and beer drinking. We weren't in a frat. We just went back to work.

Late that night, with less than 24 hours until we'd begin the mission, I remember a tough-talking officer back in the barracks, a man who wanted to be Special Forces but failed, giving me a hard time about having a light on as I studied maps and went over details for the mission. He was from South Boston. He talked tough with that rough accent where the letter "R" is all but missing. He'd tell you about how he grew up fighting other tough guys on the hard streets. He had defined himself this way and he hated the fact that I was a Green Beret and was going on a mission for which he couldn't qualify. I knew because I was in the class he had failed. I remember how stupid I found him when he pulled rank and ordered me to turn out the light. I remember how juvenile he looked when he took out a sleeping mask.

War has a way of bringing out the best and worst in people.

WE LEFT DEEP IN THE NIGHT. Stars were bright holes in the sky. The soldiers at the gate gave us a dead-eyed, set-jaw look. They could tell this mission was different. They could see we were deploying for something big.

I stood in the moving, sand-colored Humvee's gun turret with my hands on a .50-caliber machine gun. We had whisper mics attached to our helmets that would pop on if we spoke, but no one was saying a thing. Hollywood screenwriters would write some clever and macho banter for this scene, but we were professionals. We'd only speak if we needed to be heard. If anyone tried to crack a joke, or tried to fill the silence, they'd have gotten their ass handed to them. The radio network needed to stay open in case something real happened. We only spoke necessary words. The rest was managed with hand and arm signals, and actions taken without words by guys who'd done this before. This left a loud silence filled with Humvee engines and vehicle shocks shaking and tires spinning and thoughts screaming in our minds without interruption.

We were a convoy of twenty vehicles, a dozen Humvees and eight light trucks used by the ANA soldiers. We had our headlights on, and we were really moving down the highway south of Kandahar. At times like this, speed is the best defense. Still, I remember the crack of far-off rifles as the Taliban let us know the hills were theirs. I'd read and heard about Chechen snipers making long-range kills on American soldiers out in those great expanses. Someone from Arizona might think this terrain normal, but someone like me, from Tennessee, finds its openness humbling, even fearsome. Especially when we all knew most of the snipers were Chechens who'd gained their experience killing Russians, sometimes from 1,000 meters. Now they were killing Americans. Strange world.

In the truck with me was Sean, the driver. Next to him was SFC Bill Brown, the acting team sergeant in the right front (passenger) seat behind an M240 machine gun chambered in 7.62 mm (.308) NATO ammunition that was attached to a vehicular mount. Bill was a Texan. He was young, but moved fast and with a swagger usually reserved for more seasoned veterans. He would later trade his helmet for a Dallas Cowboys' ball cap during combat—his way of showing disdain and open disregard for the enemy. I feel like it also helped him hang onto who he was at times in that living hell of a battle, though it's strictly forbidden.

There was also an Air Force Joint Terminal Attack Controller (JTAC) and a junior medic in the vehicle, but I wasn't looking at either of them. I was in the gun turret, staring into darkness.

The Humvees flying along in the column held 30 Green Berets and about 50 ANA soldiers in their small pickups trailing behind. The Green Berets were split into three teams, each with a captain in charge. The Company Commander and Mission Commander on the ground was Major Jarrod Hill. There were also two other Air Force JTACs in the column. These guys are seriously high-speed Air Force dudes who direct combat aircraft engaged in close air support and other offensive air operations. NATO calls these guys "Forward Air Controllers." All during my career, I made jokes about the Air Force, because, even as a kid, I saw that on Andrews Air Force base, the Air Force had the best golf courses, swimming pools, and movie theaters. I'd never witnessed the discipline of the Air Force that I'd seen in the Army and Marines. The Air Force personnel I saw dressed and acted like FedEx employees. I used to repeat the stale joke: "I had an opportunity to join the Air Force, but I went in the military instead." These JTACs would make me regret this.

Later, I would see this JTAC sitting with a 240G Machine Gun. We were getting shot at from three directions, and everyone had white-knuckled gorilla grips on their guns. We were nearly going into muscle failure from aggressive shooting as we tried to kill the attacking enemy, but this JTAC wasn't touching his machine gun. He was communicating by laptop and radio to incoming aircraft. Bullets were hitting the sides of the vehicles. Guns were pounding, and brass was splashing over the sides of the Humvees, but he knew close air support would do more to keep us alive than his machine gun. It took balls not to shoot. He let mouth-breathing cavemen like me shoot the machine guns. Not that he didn't know how. It took remarkable self-control to talk in the air support, instead. It took a deep understanding that he was a part of a team, and that it was his job not to shoot, but to guide in the air support, unless there were no air assets available.

I stood in that machine-gun turret for untold hours. Our twelve Humvees led the way. In the rear were Toyota Hilux four-wheel drive trucks with mounted machine guns. The ANA soldiers were just piled on them. There were eight or more ANA soldiers in each pickup.

All of us had mixed feelings about the ANA soldiers. We'd have two mission meetings, one with and one without them. I saw them do very brave things. I also saw them do very undisciplined, and even stupid, things. But that's the perspective of a Special Force's soldier with some pretty good schooling and training. They simply didn't have all that training to weed out the bad and to grow the good into great soldiers. We knew there were always active Taliban contacts within our ANA forces, and it is difficult for an American to understand all of the family and tribal alliances that influence the ANA soldiers. So they're hard to read, and even harder to trust. Still, we were fighting for the same cause, so we did our best to know and fight with them.

As we drove through the darkness to a point where we'd go off road, I remember thinking about Tom Maholik, a Green Beret who was shot in the head and killed in a firefight in Afghanistan. We'd worked together in SWC. He was running an intel course and I was managing the students in our medical course. We had collaborated on different training projects. We even ran a relay for charity together. Each member on our team ran five miles. There were 12 relay members. We ran from Fort Bragg, North Carolina, to Arlington National Cemetery to raise money for the children of fallen soldiers. Tom then made E8 and took charge of an A-Team. Soon after, he was killed. This hit me hard. I'd already lost students—some on their first missions. Quality people. You can't quantify those losses. Each one was as talented as Pat Tillman, but just weren't as well known. It's amazing how much we put into people only to have them get killed.

Tom was a soft-spoken, nice human being. If you had met him back in the States, you'd never have thought he was a Green Beret. But you just never know what's in a person until you push and test them, until you see what their potential is. So, yeah, I wanted a chance to avenge him. That's natural, I guess. He was a short guy with thunder thighs, strawberry blond hair, and a stubbornness that had pushed him through things that had broken most. Tom came to me in the dark as I stood silently in that gun turret. Others did too. Those are the only times when you can let your mind open to the past when you're on the enemy's side of the line.

When the sun began to glow on the eastern horizon, I could see the haze of our headlights just touching the edges of the brown hills. I saw that it wasn't as flat as far as the eyes can see. A light line on the horizon showed mountain ranges. Our vehicles shut off their headlights. We were getting close to going off-road into a Taliban-occupied area.

Before it was full light, we turned off the pavement near the southern edge of the Red Desert. We stopped the vehicles in splayed-out fighting formation—each facing out. All around were big red sand dunes looking majestic in the early light. Some of us stepped out to form a perimeter. Under our boots was the softest sand you can imagine. Like stepping in dry snow.

We had to lower the tire pressure so the vehicles could handle the sand, and we needed to relieve ourselves before we started into Indian country. I don't say that with any disrespect, but that is how we talked. And it is a good metaphor. We were like a cavalry patrol hunting Geronimo, hoping not to end up like General George Armstrong Custer did at the Battle of Little Bighorn, all the while not knowing that metaphor would almost come true in just a few days.

We had vacant, serious expressions on our faces as we stared into the Red Desert, looking for the enemy. All we had to fall back on was one another, the A-Team cemented by our Green Beret training, and, hopefully, air support. We would soon need all three.

WE STARTED INTO THE SOFT SAND of the Red Desert. Now, if this were a Hollywood production, there would be theme music—something loud and pounding—and there would be snippets of soldiers behind machine guns, and you probably would have thought it was all so macho. In the Hollywood version, there would be an endless dialogue of crass one-liners from men going to battle. But, in this real version, there was nothing but the sounds of engines and tires in deep sand and the concern that a teammate wasn't deep enough in the turret to avoid a clear sniper shot.

We had to stop to dig the Humvees out of the soft, red sand again and again. Over the next couple days, there was this growing tension. In a classic cavalry Western, some Indian scout would see smoke signals on the horizon and would find a burning wagon train with arrows in it. Here, we saw the dust from the vehicles getting closer. One night, we watched many sets of headlights from Taliban vehicles closing in slowly, eerily.

There were several ambushes and a few minor wounds to our men over those first few days. We passed through a village where we could feel the attack coming. These villages have adobe walls built to defend themselves against the Russians. They'd funnel you into bottlenecks. In that terrain, you can't avoid those places. We had the feeling we simply got there faster than they expected. They wanted to attack, but weren't ready.

There was one stupid delay when the ANA troops refused to proceed. It took a little while for us to figure out why. They had run out of cigarettes and wanted us to call in an airdrop. They didn't care what it would cost. They didn't care that it was leaving us exposed to attack. We had no choice but to comply. These are the sorts of things that can eat away at even an A-Team. We called in the emergency cigarette drop, established a perimeter, and waited.

Over the next few days, there were a few contacts with the enemy that resulted in short, but intense, gunfights as we got closer to Sperwan Ghar in the Panjwayi district in the Kandahar Province. But the real fight started that fourth day when we could see the hill named Sperwan Ghar but had to pull back three kilometers before it got dark and we all but ran out of ammo.

After that eerie night out in the wide open, and just after sunrise, we went right back into the hornet's nest. We were ready to go long before sunrise. We knew the "stand to" principle. This comes from battles between Native Americans and the white man in the Old West. The settlers, and even their troops, more often than not, weren't in tune with the environment. The Native American was. Native Americans would use the elements to be ready before daylight, which, as any hunter knows, comes at least 30 minutes before sunrise. Out in the flat, wide-open desert, it comes even earlier. "Stand to" is the practice of standing up and getting ready before even the first red hint of light begins to grow.

We deviated slightly from the course we had taken the day before to avoid IEDs (Improvised Explosive Devices), but the terrain dictated a certain general course. We crept in slowly, expecting the hornet's nest to explode, but it was so quiet, a scary sort of quiet. To continue the Old West metaphor, there were tumbleweeds blowing by. This was ghost-town spooky. We had reports from air support telling us there was a beehive of activity ahead of us. We went in knowing we were greatly outnumbered, but, since the first weeks of the war, the Taliban hadn't tried to challenge us with numbers, so command just didn't see the Custer's Last Stand scene coming.

As we crept in, we stopped often to make listening halts. We'd stop, shut down the vehicles, and sit quietly, listening. We didn't hear anything. As we closed in on what we later learned was a school turned into a Taliban training camp, we stopped within 400 meters of Sperwan Ghar, which stood like a Pyramid just over the village and the Taliban training camp.

We sent ten soldiers up the hill. I was behind, in the gun turret of my Humvee. As a medic, I knew they wouldn't send me out in front; they prefer to keep a medic close to the front, but not right in the most intense action. The ten soldiers reached the top of Sperwan Ghar without incident, but one of the ANA soldiers tripped a landmine. Special Forces are trained not to touch things that look different. You look for ground that has been recently turned over. You don't just poke around. This ANA soldier saw something and decided to see what it was. The explosion didn't kill him, but it woke the hornet's nest.

Suddenly, the bad guys were coming out of the ground. They were using adobe walls as cover to close in. The voices from the Green Berets on the hill were desperate. They were about to be overrun. This might be a Custer's Last Stand, after all.

Our vehicle was ordered to drive up the hill so I could give them cover to fall back by shooting over their heads with the .50-caliber machine gun.

We went up a dirt track, which was the only way up. Sean kept the vehicle moving carefully in the tracks of a previous vehicle. We'd already dealt with the wounded Afghan soldier, and now we needed to get up there to back up our brothers who were getting pinned down.

Halfway up the hill, an IED was detonated under our Humvee. I was lit on fire, and there were holes punched through my body. The detonation launched Sean 70 feet away onto the hill beside us, miraculously without major injury.

I could feel my legs burning. I tried to climb out of the turret, but my leg was broken. Bone shards stuck out of my pants leg. I collapsed. I remember seeing the sand popping up from the ground around my face. I thought this strange and didn't for a moment realize these were bullets striking the ground next to me. My leg was almost detached. A piece of shrapnel the size of a baseball had gone through me. I was still being burned alive.

Army Staff Sgt. Jude Voss came running to help. Despite the fact that he could be killed by the incoming bullets from Taliban fighters' AK-47s, PKM machine guns, and rocket-propelled grenades, he pulled me out of the fire and yanked me into a ditch. He and others then carried me farther from the battle to a ditch alongside a nearby marijuana field and began administering medical care. Taliban continued to move in on us. I remember thinking: *I've never even smoked this stuff, but now I'm going to die in it?*

Captain Bradley had found Sean and pulled him out of harm's way. Sean couldn't believe he basically wasn't injured.

As I lay bleeding in that ditch, somehow I stayed conscious and kept helping the guys working on me. "I'm bleeding here," I'd say and helped them to apply pressure, bandages, and even a tourniquet that—without question—saved my life. A junior medic was fumbling and nervous and I had to help him. He later matured into the primary instructor for trauma in the Special Operations Medic program, but, at the time, he was very green and obviously nervous. The things that have turned him into one of the world's best and strongest people are things I wouldn't wish on anyone. I salute that guy.

A one-pound piece of shrapnel had penetrated my hip and thigh and had continued to travel through my pelvis and abdomen. The shrapnel injury, burns, and other wounds I received before being rescued were devastating. I remember my Green Beret buddies asking how I was as the fight waged all around and Air Force planes dropped bombs on Taliban positions close enough to shake the ground where I lay. Every time someone asked how I was, the medic would give a quick sign by moving his fingers in a straight line near his throat to indicate I didn't have a chance.

I felt that if I was to have any chance, I was going to have to help *them* save *me*. The men followed my instructions. Somehow, a brave helicopter pilot managed to land and pull me out. The battle raged for another eight hours. Eventually, the Taliban were all killed or scattered. Reports vary, but many agree that as many as 1,000 Taliban were killed in the Battle of Sperwan Ghar.

For his actions on September 5, 2006, Jude Voss received the Silver Star, the third highest medal given for distinctive gallantry. I remember telling Voss, "You are a friend of mine for life, whether you like it or not."

You may be wondering how these actions from a team of Green Berets in a war zone are relevant to you. Though most of us don't have to face life-or-death decisions, we do need to build our teams as fathers or mothers, colleagues and bosses, patients or doctors, students and teachers. Accomplishing the goals in each mission in our lives means utilizing the same framework an A-Team does.

No matter what your goal—beating cancer, starting a company, getting a degree—you need to attack that goal as the head of or part of a team. The decision to do this, and to tackle any other opportunity or problem in life, requires a strong answer from us on why we should tackle the challenge. As a Special Forces' soldier, many times I have found myself in places where people were trying to kill me. Later, in business, my competitors wanted to trounce me in the marketplace, and, during my many surgeries after being badly wounded on the battlefield, I found myself struggling to survive and asking if it was worth the struggle. These are questions all our wounded warriors, and anyone with an addiction, disease, or other dilemma, faces. All of these problems require a real decision and a real answer; without a real answer, we are going to quit on ourselves. I've seen this many times in the Green Berets, in the hospital, and in life.

To understand the course of action necessary to making this decision, I need to take you to the dark place I went to next.

2

THE CODE

What You Live By Is What Others Follow

"The feeling of commiseration is the beginning of humanity;
the feeling of shame and dislike is the beginning of righteousness;
the feeling of deference and compliance is the beginning of propriety;
and the feeling of right and wrong is the beginning of wisdom.
Men have these four beginnings just as they have their four limbs.
Having these four beginnings, but saying that they cannot develop
them is to destroy themselves."

—MENCIUS, CHINA, THIRD CENTURY, B.C.

You think about a lot of things when you're in a hospital bed with tubes in you and pieces of your body sewn back on, all the while knowing you really should be dead. At first, how you judge yourself is the worst of it. You are a Green Beret with 18 years experience, and you are physically tough and have all these skills you've earned in sweat and blood. Then you find you'd only worked to harden the parts that are now blown up and burned away. You find that everything you need to *really* be strong is undeveloped and little understood, and that mainstream society, and even the Army, doesn't grasp any of this.

Answers are fleeting in these early and agonizing hours. You are charred and stitched back together and no one can yet say if you'll live or die. Machines are beeping along with your vital signs. You hear them and can't move. You are gagging on the smell of your own burned flesh. You are as helpless and as close to death as a newborn delivered prematurely. You are flat on your back and can't see your feet and hope they are still there. You begin to loathe your weak body and to feel so desperately sorry for yourself. When the nurses turn the lights off at night, you lay looking up into the dark, and part of you begins to whisper that *you should die.*

Then you realize that how you see your body isn't the worst of it.

The first to come to the hospital was my wife. She came into my hospital room in San Antonio just a day after I'd arrived and after the first of 17 surgical procedures. She had a white gown over her clothes, a white cap over her hair, and a white facemask covering her mouth and nose. My wounds were so fresh and open, anything could infect me, so everyone wore these things before they came into my private room. This is especially the case on a burn ward.

When she walked in, I looked across the room and into her eyes. They were moist and wide and were expanding from gut-wrenching horror, and then she was falling, falling forward. I tried to reach for her. I couldn't move. My left arm tried to go up. My torso tried to sit up. None of that was possible. I fell back with pain smashing through my convulsing body as she landed face down on the tile floor with a fleshy thud. This was a preview of coming attractions, as I wouldn't be helping anyone for a long time, not even myself.

Pain crashed through me like jolts of electricity. The torment that I couldn't help my wife rattled me deep below where the flesh hurts. I couldn't even help her off the floor. I wasn't a man anymore. I was just some destroyed piece of flesh lying on white sheets.

She was out cold and face down on the tile floor, and no nurse even noticed. I called out, and the heaving of my chest and gut almost made me pass out. I frantically tapped the call button with my right index finger for a nurse; it seemed like forever before anyone responded. Time went so slowly. I was dying inside knowing she was down there, and I couldn't do a damn thing about it.

Finally, a nurse came into the room and helped my wife off the floor. She took her from the room by holding her right arm and waist as someone does for a very drunk person.

My wife knew what had happened, but nothing could have prepared her for how I looked. Part of my abdomen was so swollen that it was resting on a table pushed up to the edge of my bed. I was covered in bandages. I still had my legs and arms, but one of my legs had to have been virtually sewn back on as the compound fracture was so complete.

My wife, Donna, would later write in her journal: "Why had I passed out the first time I saw him? Why? Nervous? Thinking it wasn't him? I didn't want to believe it was."

Donna first heard I was wounded at 2:30 a.m. a few days before. She had been up with our 18-month-old son, Gregory, off and on all night. Gregory was restless and was saying my name, and she'd had a nightmare about me. Then the phone rang.

It was Lieutenant Colonel Leo Ruth, commander of the 96th Civil Affairs Battalion. He called to tell her I'd been wounded, and that he didn't know how badly, but he would call back soon. The next call was from the wife of another Green Beret. She'd gotten an email about me from her husband, who was stationed in Kandahar. She told my wife I was dead. Soon, another wife called and said I'd lost all my limbs. The calls kept coming. The wives were repeating rumors gleaned by people listening to radio reports from the battlefield and secondhand stories from Kandahar. People in Afghanistan, but far from the still-raging battle, were repeating rumors that grew in proportion as they passed from one person to another. They were like children playing telephone with my wife's sanity. Dad always said not to miss an opportunity to keep your mouth shut. This was one.

My wife was delirious with panic and despair. Her parents happened to be staying with her. They did what they could to help her and to take care of Gregory, but the phone kept ringing.

At 7 a.m., Colonel Ruth came to our home near Fort Bragg, North Carolina. He said he was there to answer the phone. He'd heard what had been happening and was outraged. He was there to tell all the well-meaning wives to stop calling. He answered the phone every time it rang and told them what they were doing to Donna. He told her I was alive and had been taken from the battlefield by helicopter to Kandahar. He said if I was stable, I'd soon be sent to Germany.

In those early and dramatic hours, Donna was going to fly to Germany. She didn't have the money for the flights, and the Army didn't have the programs they now do to handle any of this, so Colonel

Ruth used his credit card to buy her a ticket. She never used it, though, as I was soon moved to a plane headed for the States.

My Army medical team needed a burn unit to fly with me from Germany. They didn't have one. But, by chance, Dr. Dave Barillo—a doctor at the Brooke Army Medical Center in San Antonio—was there to teach a course on caring for burn victims. Dr. Barillo volunteered to fly with me to keep me alive. He was proud that he was helping a Green Beret. As we flew, he kept me conscious by talking about guns and shooting recreationally, and anything else in common he could think of to keep me awake. When we landed at Andrew's Air Force Base just outside Washington, D.C., he let me use his cell phone to call Donna.

We didn't say much. I was very weak, and she was in pieces.

Soon we were flying again to a burn center in San Antonio. Dr. Barillo kept talking to me about things that had nothing to do with war or death. He kept me awake and fighting for life.

A day later, and after a few minutes of being walked back and forth by a nurse outside my hospital room, Donna began to regain her balance. She came in and apologized. She was crying. Her face was bruised from the fall, and this made me more upset than my own wounds. She shrugged it off and began to do what she could for me. She was adjusting. Before long, she would become my everything. She was strong in ways I wasn't, and I had to learn this from her. I thought I was among the toughest breed alive, yet there she was, teaching me the feminine virtues of strength we often don't see or understand today.

Soon, my father came. He has passed now and is buried at Arlington, but when he comes up in conversation—and he often does—people still affectionately call him "Chief Stube," as he had retired from the U.S. Navy. I'll never forget this cryptic conversation my father had with the head surgeon as I lay on the hospital bed.

The doctor said to my father, "Sir, your son has lost a lot of intestines."

My dad said, "That's good."

I managed to say through the pain and drugs they were pumping into me, "That's not good."

My father looked at my swollen midsection, where a piece of shrapnel four inches wide had been taken out of me, and said, "Look at it this way, son: Now you don't have the guts to go back to Afghanistan."

This was so much the right thing to say. I wanted to laugh, but it hurt too much.

Looking back, I'd say that my father knew from experience how to act. He'd been badly burned while serving in the Navy. He was the only one to survive a horrifying accident on a ship. During the Vietnam War, an ensign had flipped the wrong switch near a jet engine. Hydraulic fluid sprayed everyone. It lit on fire and became a flamethrower. Five people died almost instantly. When my father stood up, his palms stuck to the metal deck and the skin from his elbows to his fingertips slid off like rubber gloves. Medics tried to help him, but he pushed them away with his skinless hands. He kept fighting them off as he walked to sickbay.

When he walked into sickbay, there was a young medic there, and my father said, "Hey kid, you got a Band-Aid?"

My father never told me that story. I heard it from another Navy man who'd seen the whole thing. That was how my dad lived. He was Chief Stube to the day he died. Though my dad was medically discharged from the Navy after that accident, he re-entered the U.S. Military later and completed nearly 30 years of service to his country.

As we talked, my father reminded me that George Washington's image is on the Purple Heart. Washington, that man, that general, that President who stood up bravely under fire so many times and who kept the course for freedom as his army starved and struggled even to find enough boots during harsh winters at Valley Forge, is on the Purple Heart. He explained that Washington didn't want to be President and that he willingly left the White House and peacefully passed the reins of power after just two terms—setting an example of what someone who believes in things greater than himself does. Now we think of that as a normal thing, but, at the time, it could have gone much differently were it not for Washington's character. My father said that the selfless ideals Washington lived by had also helped save him when he'd been burned on that ship.

After telling that story, he said, "Son, you no doubt remember me telling you that if you want sympathy, you'll find it in the dictionary between 'shit' and 'syphilis.' "

I nodded and tried to smile. It had been one of the points of view that shaped my childhood.

He said, "Here's something else. I need you to know now that sympathy may pay well in the short term, but if you cash in on sympathy, it will take everything from you in the long run."

He didn't say anymore. Instead of preaching, he liked to let profound stuff like that sink in. As he said this, I wanted to raise my chin and square my shoulders as I lay all swollen, burned, full of holes, and gutted by shrapnel. But, honestly, it would take many more months before I realized what he meant by being careful with sympathy. Pity will suck your strength and kill your manhood. If you become addicted to it, and many do, sympathy will grow like a disease, like an alcoholic's need for a drink, until your body and mind aren't well without it. Soon, maybe before you are even aware of it, pity will define you, and you won't like yourself for this. Other people feel the same. People are repulsed by this condition, even if they don't know why, even though they'll never say so out loud. A person with this addiction to sympathy loses their identity. They lose their pride and self-reliance. They die.

All that was to come. At this desperate hour, I was sinking, falling into an abyss of being nothing I knew anymore. I was a dead body that was somehow still awake, and I was screaming in my head that I shouldn't be here. I should be under a gravestone in Arlington that my wife and, someday, son could put flowers next to on Memorial Day weekends as they called me a hero and shed a tear before moving on with their lives.

I thought on this as I looked up at that bare hospital ceiling and smelled my burned flesh. I realized I couldn't even come up with a good definition of what a hero was, so how did I know I even was one or if they would even think of me that way? All I knew was that whatever I had been was blown away. I honestly couldn't even define *what* I had lost aside from the physical things. If I couldn't define what was lost, how could I get back on my feet?

I was in this confused state of mind when an Army liaison from Fort Bragg came to see me. He said he flew from North Carolina to Texas to help me readjust and to tell me the Army was there for me.

I asked, "Readjust to what?"

He gave me a puzzled look. He tried again and said, "You ain't finished." He said that there was something else.

I listened, but he had no concrete things to tell me. He had reached the limit of his understanding for how I felt. All he knew was that healthy men and women in his command didn't ask questions like that. If they do, they are told to get with the program. If they don't, they are gone. He knew that the young men and women in his command were so busy defining themselves as soldiers, they weren't asking things like who they were or what their lives were about. He thought that whatever questions they had about their paths in life were being satisfied by their roles as soldiers and parents and other things. He knew that people who ask questions like that often leave the Army. He had seen in the past that such people blow with the wind until they settle somewhere and hopefully answer such questions for themselves. Or maybe they never do and just drown in a bottle or who knows what? He knew that much. And he knew he didn't want that for me.

I got quiet then. I didn't want to give this person a hard time. I wanted to give him the impression that I was as strong as ever. I wanted to thank him for all he did and was doing by putting on a good face. What I needed was simply something he didn't have to give. The code had worked for me when I was on active duty, but now I needed something more, something that the best teams everywhere need. Still, he was a good man. I remember him, months later, telling our nurses I was going home for Christmas to be with my wife and child. My nurses gave him these "No, he isn't" expressions, but he made sure it happened. It wasn't easy, but it was a step toward normalcy. It was a step we were only able to take because Donna had become such a pro at cleaning my wounds.

I was deep in this melancholy when Bruce Fracier, a Green Beret brother, came to see me. He told the nurses out in a waiting area as he suited up before coming in to see me: "Stube has killed more people than smallpox." He had meant this as a great compliment. He thought it was a cool thing to say. At any other time, it would be great team-room talk. It would be seen as true street cred for a professional warrior. It was cool to him and to most. It would have been to me too—before I was blown up, shot, and left lying on a bed in a burn unit.

The thing was, hearing him say I had killed more people than smallpox as I was thinking about the men I'd killed, was a different thing. I wanted to know what the men I had killed had been like. What did their families look like? Did they have children? Were they volunteers or were they forced to fight? I still didn't know if I would live or die, and the prospect of meeting them and God frightened me. Bruce just had no way of knowing the warrior part of me had been slain, and that I was trying to become something else. Weeks before, I would have puffed up my chest at those words, and I would have driven on with no introspection. Now I was wondering why I had been spared, and if I should try to go on.

After Bruce left, Dr. Barillo affectionately repeated the smallpox line. Other people did too. They said this line, and I wouldn't smile. When they got to my room, they wouldn't find a bold warrior; they would find a humbled man trying to come to terms with what he'd done. They'd get solemn when they saw me grimace. I hoped I wasn't insulting them, as they meant well, but I just couldn't fake a smile about such things anymore.

The image of the indestructible warrior I'd long lived by was dead. I felt dead. I felt as if I were a corpse, and that my spirit was floating around the room, seeing all these unseeing people and wondering why they didn't see me.

I was just beginning to understand that people who've lived like I had for all those years aren't whole. I was starting to understand how shallow I'd been. I was beginning to see there are two halves to what makes a person whole, to complete a real code for success in life. It would take a lot more pain and trouble before I would understand any of this.

I began to ask for chaplains. I always wanted one there. I know people get like that when they're near death or in some bad spot in life, and I'd always thought that was weak. I used to make fun of people like that. *Oh, I'm sick, time to turn to God. Oh, I'm old, time to turn to God.*

Perhaps it can be superficial and desperate like that, but I found there is much more to it than this.

There were worse things. In the coming weeks, I would suffer a heart attack during one of my surgeries. During it all, I couldn't understand *how* I had lived. *How* does a person live through the wounds I'd received? My friend and Green Beret brother, Nate Chapman, took one small bullet in the thigh and died. How did I live? I was a medic in the Green Berets and had done a lot of work on wounded soldiers. In medic school at Fort Bragg, we trained by replicating war wounds, so I knew what kills and what someone can live through. I knew very well that I should be dead. Everyone on the battlefield thought so too. As we had waited for the helicopter to take me out of the raging firefight with hundreds of Taliban, I heard soldiers ask about me, and I saw a medic shake his fingers in front of his throat. This is the sign that a person doesn't have a chance. I would see this again on the helicopter and again in Kandahar. It followed me like a bad habit that is contagiously spread from one person to the next. From my training, I'd learned not to do that as a patient can often see, hear, and perceive more than we think. Seeing a gesture like that doesn't help a patient's psychological disposition.

The first moment of light came when a nurse in Kandahar, a woman with this charming and open way of speaking, entered the recovery room as I regained consciousness. She walked toward me holding a large chunk of jagged steel (which had passed through my hip, groin, and abdomen) up in the air and said, "Well, at least they spared the bollocks!"

I hadn't even thought about that. I wanted to laugh. Still, I was getting those looks. No one thought I had a chance. This is why I asked the chaplains why I'd lived. They said I couldn't know that. I said I wanted to do all I could to pay God back for my survival. They said I couldn't repay God, and that I was arrogant for thinking I could.

I didn't know what they meant. I told a priest to just give it to me straight.

He said, "How can I when you're so blinded by your arrogance you can't even see?"

I had asked for this stern treatment. That kind of intimacy brought straight talk, the kind I'd grown comfortable with from the Army, but, mostly, from Chief Stube.

My father was sitting quietly in the room when the priest said that to me in a tone usually reserved for unruly children. My father sat up. He'd brought me up in the Christian church, but fell away from the church when he was near death from wounds he'd received in the Navy. He was in a Navy hospital in Japan when his wife left him and abandoned their children—my half brothers and sisters—without telling anyone why. She just left. This was in the early 1970s, before the Internet made finding and connecting with people so easily possible. It would be years before he found all of his children again.

When my father came to see me in the hospital in 2006, he still hadn't come all the way back into the church. So when the priest said this to me, my father didn't say anything. The priest left after asking me to pray and telling me the answers would show themselves, that all I had to do was open my eyes to see.

As weeks went by, all the doctors kept calling me a miracle. Among the staff of nurses and therapists, my nickname was "Freakshow." The brutal nature of the burn care and wound scrubbing is a rapid way to build relationships with folks—good and bad. This would be illuminated by a couple of personalities involved in my care.

The priests kept telling me I should be thankful and I should do what I could to live my life with God. I didn't know or perceive the exact context they had in mind, and I sometimes resented their evasive answers, though I had literally begged for their presence and counsel. It would take much more time before I would understand what they were trying to tell me. I needed to find a real foundation—one I'd superficially skipped over as a Green Beret who had thought he could stomp out any enemy—before any of that would make sense.

My wife adjusted and started to work on me. She left our infant son with her parents. She was a young wife who'd left her young child to care for her wounded husband. This was even harder than I knew. It took her a month to learn all the medical necessities for cleaning my wounds, but she committed herself to this. I was her full-time job, and I wasn't easy to get along with. I was wrestling with things and was so confused. When a nurse worked on me, I'd man up and take the pain. When Donna worked on changing my bandages, I'd tell her she was doing it wrong. I'd say things to her I wouldn't to anyone else. I was so vile to her. It was easy to blame her for the pain I felt in those moments, though I'd never done that to any of the hospital staff. I guess it's true what they say: "We only hurt the ones we love."

I fell into a deep depression. I couldn't even go to the bathroom. My wife had to clean me. I thought I had nothing and was done in life. When Donna saw me giving up, at first she became very quiet. But then, one morning, she came in with a life and energy I'd never seen directed toward me before. She wouldn't back off. This made me angry. It was easy for me to say she didn't understand. I got nasty.

She then did something that woke me up.

She was pushing my wheelchair, taking me to physical therapy (that I didn't want to do), when she suddenly stopped, walked in front of me, and put her hands in the air, palms facing me. She looked down at me with her wet, almost crying eyes. I didn't know if she was going to scream or cry when she said, "Greg, I'm not doing this for me. You won't ever be happy if you don't do all you can to beat this."

I got quiet then. I thought this was a trite thing to say, but I wasn't so sure whether it was or not. The way she said it was so honest and powerful it shook me. I didn't know how to respond. My lack of conviction startled me. This wasn't what I was like. I always just drove on. I knew what to do, and I did it. Now I didn't know who I was or what I should drive on *to*.

Donna told me I had to find the strength for her and for our son and for so many others. I nodded. I was still a Frankenstein thing all sewn together, and I still had a hole in my side that wasn't healing where that pound-and-a-half piece of metal had gutted me. I had tubes, lines, bags, and small pumps and machines that had to go everywhere I did. I still didn't have a self-identity I could see, at least, nothing I recognized. But she was right, or I thought she must be. I got quiet and knew I had a lot to learn. This is when I began to have visions of the many who had gone before me and thrived, despite these conditions, and worse. I was back in the Green Beret selection process again, in some sick way, and a big part of me wanted to make the cut.

While Donna stayed strong, we saw more than one wife come in and read divorce notices to their wounded husbands. We heard about wounded warriors we'd gotten to know in the hospital who went home and hanged or shot themselves. They weren't growing past their wounded bodies. They couldn't adjust. All they knew were the physical and superficial, and now that was gone. Ours is a society that puts the self at the center of the universe. People live as if self-gratification is everything. Pain is pitied and managed away. Our elderly are hidden from us. Our wounded are given sympathy and attention to distract them, but they are rarely given what they really need. I saw signs of this superficiality all around me. I was just beginning to see what was wrong, not with my body, but with my conception of myself.

At this time, one of my nurses became cruel. She was an older woman, and you could tell she'd always been attractive. She defined herself by her looks and what they did to men. She liked to flirt with her patients and wanted that recognition of being an attractive woman even from the most gruesomely wounded soldiers. She wanted me to treat her like she was beautiful. She wanted me to flirt back with her. If I didn't respond to her in those ways, she would turn as cold as a block of ice and become very unpleasant. I was flat on my back and healing and was such a burned and swollen mess I couldn't give her what she wanted. Anyway, I reserve that behavior for my wife. When I wouldn't flirt back, she became mean. Her self-identity was superficial. She had dyed red hair and an overly made-up face as she tried desperately to look young. I wasn't acknowledging her for her looks, so she began punishing me for this. She began to change my bandages in vicious ways. She began to withhold pain medication. I saw that she would only put a partial dose into my IV line.

Now, realize that, at the time, I'd become addicted to pain meds. We all do in that situation. It is human. Knowing this was happening elevated my awareness of my own pain and weakness. I wanted to fight this physical need, this weakness, but it's not easy to fight when you are flat on your back and still healing.

Then she got rough. If I asked about her suddenly rough manner, she would be curt and turn her back and walk out. That was my nurse for the night. I would lie there and suffer if I didn't play her game. I didn't want to complain. I didn't want to be labeled a problem; all the nurses might treat me differently then. She was living so superficially— as I had for so long as a Green Beret—that real human compassion was beyond her.

Meanwhile, the Army's attempt to provide care continuity was to assign case managers. These were basically social workers. They understood the bureaucratic process, but not what really mattered. They treated me as if I were a child. I was a senior noncommissioned officer in the Special Forces with more schooling and leadership experience then they'd ever see, but they treated me like some abused child who was a ward of the state. I couldn't break through their superficial and very bureaucratic point of view. To them, I was just another one of those wounded men they had to deal with. They wouldn't look me in the eyes and try to see me for who I was. They absolutely refused to give me credit for anything I might have done before becoming a professional patient. This infuriated me. I'd seldom witnessed this kind of condescension, even as a buck private in the infantry. Some thought of themselves as if they were some kind of parole officer, gladly scaling back my freedoms. What a God complex.

Then, one day, Donna and I saw the wife of a wounded soldier walking from our quarters to the hospital across the street. She was wearing pajamas. We both criticized her lack of decorum. We thought she should keep a better appearance for her wounded husband and for the military community. But then, we found out that her husband had died of his wounds and that she had come running out of the bed. She was so distraught that what she was wearing didn't matter.

We fell apart when we learned this. We detested ourselves for thinking such judgmental things. How dare we judge her? How did we know what she'd gone through, who she was, and what was happening? We were thinking just as superficially as that mean nurse and those caseworkers.

This was when we turned a corner together. This was when faith began to heal us.

Donna and I both made a conscious effort to stop judging others and ourselves superficially. This new way of seeing things made me begin to hate the phrase "wounded warrior." I get it. It's graphic and real. Some of our warriors come back with parts missing and with holes shot right through them. But that's just their body; it's not them. When I learned to suspend judgement and open my eyes to the truth, that there is something special in us that is more important than our bodies, I began to heal. It took all but losing my body for me to understand this. All of what happened to me and what was killing those around me settled into a theme that suddenly showed what I needed, and what anyone who gets lost in war or in life really needs.

The code I'd lived my life by as a Green Beret soldier was no longer enough. I needed these deeper—what I call "feminine"—virtues to become a complete person who could climb out of that hospital bed and create new A-Teams to tackle the next physical and mental challenges in my personal and professional life.

Whatever your goal, before you can build or join a team, you have to know your values, your code. If you don't, you will be uncertain of yourself. People will sense this in you, and they won't follow you if you are unsure of what you're following.

I discovered that I was not my tough-guy persona, or even my physical body, when I was in the hospital. I'd spent my life living the warrior's code, and now I was entering a new and deeper phase of life, looking at myself as something other than my body, and also at those around me as something apart from their appearances. Before you can build your team—in personal relationships and in business—you need to know these two halves of yourself.

Next comes your call to action.

3

THE CALL TO LEAD

Leadership Must Occur at Every Step
in a Chain of Command

"The greatest leader is not necessarily the one who does the greatest
things. He is the one that gets the people to do the greatest things."

—RONALD REAGAN

There is an age-old debate about whether a leader is born or made.
This is the wrong question to ask. First, it is neither one nor the
other, but is, of course, both. More importantly, thinking of the question
in this way misses the whole, underlying basis of leadership. A leader
is made of good steel that is forged in action—by the mistakes, failures,
and triumphs learned by doing. But, ideally, that action shouldn't be
war or bankruptcy. These hard lessons should be learned in training,
where the cost is only painful to your ego, or maybe a little to your body
or career prospects—if you don't have even a little skin in the game, the
lessons aren't real enough to do their hard work.

There is a brutal example of this in Sun Tzu's *The Art of War*, an
ancient Chinese text that is seen as mandatory reading in many ROTC
classes and the war colleges run by the U.S. Military. I am referring
to the story of King Ho-lú and his concubines. King Ho-lú wanted a
demonstration of Sun Tzu's theories of war. So the king tells Sun Tzu to
turn his concubines, some 300 women, into effective troops for him to
inspect. The concubines were summoned and divided into two companies. Sun Tzu placed one of the king's two favorite concubines in charge

of each company and gave the women armor and weapons while carefully explaining a set of drills he wished them to perform.

After Sun Tzu showed the women what he wished them to do, he ordered the king's favorite concubines to lead their companies in performing the maneuvers. The concubines giggled and smiled and treated the whole thing like a big joke. Sun Tzu then repeated his orders clearly and asked them once again to do as ordered. But, again, the concubines laughed and moved about like schoolchildren. At this point, Sun Tzu said, "If the instructions are not clear, if the orders are not obeyed, it is the fault of the general. But if the instructions are clear and the soldiers still do not obey, it is the fault of their officers."

Sun Tzu then ordered an executioner to come forward and told him to behead the two concubines he'd put in charge. At this point, King Ho-lú intervenes and tells Sun Tzu that these are his favorite concubines and he would like them to be spared. But Sun Tzu replies that a general, when in the field, is autonomous. Sun Tzu then goes through with the executions. He puts two more concubines in charge of the "troops" and again orders the drill to be completed. This time, the remaining concubines perform the exercise flawlessly.

That anecdote from Sun Tzu is so extreme it is hard to forget, which is part of the point. Any modern reader will no doubt conclude that a simple demotion—and, perhaps, a physical punishment, such as being forced to run miles with a rifle held at port arms—should have the same effect without killing two people and destroying the morale of those left.

Nevertheless, the point is clear. For each team member to learn to lead and to follow, they must have skin in the game, even during practice sessions. This is fundamental to how the Green Berets create leaders.

The fact that controlled action forges a leader is something the U.S. Military knows well, but this is a lesson the business community often fails to understand. It is often just too politically incorrect for a manager to even ponder putting his or her team through practice trials that have real consequences for their team members. Instead, most companies simply try to hire managers who have been trained in action at another company. This is a gamble. This would be like the U.S. Military recruiting soldiers from foreign governments and just assuming they have the same training, protocols, ethics, and more.

If UPS hires a manager away from FedEx, they are getting someone raised in the culture found in FedEx. This can be good or bad, but it can be hard to know how another company's corporate culture has affected the new hire. He or she might bring bad habits, poor training, and more to your team. They can also bring new ways of thinking and tactics and give you insights into your corporate adversaries. But to use and recognize all of these potential problems and opportunities, you need a well-trained, established corporate culture that is open all the way up the chain of command, and that is, at the same time, too loyal to leak information or tactics back to previous employers or friends at competitors. That's a lot to ask, so it must be shown by example and enforced cleanly and fairly.

As you do this, you need a team that either knows they're the best or that knows they soon will be. To create this type of culture, the U.S. Army defines leadership as how a soldier influences others in an effort to accomplish an objective while providing purpose, direction, and motivation to those they are leading or working with. The Army tempers this with what it calls "the battlefield challenge." This is a key that unlocks how we can all achieve more. The battlefield challenge shows how we can be the kind of leaders that people want to follow, regardless of the type of authority we hold. It can allow us to possess multiple forms of authority with people we are leading or following.

The textbook stuff is important in order to give people a common basis and mutually understandable definitions of terms, but it's the action within the battlefield challenge that forges or develops real leadership traits. In the Special Forces, the battlefield challenge begins like this:

One night a call to action came in for me at 9 p.m. Thirty minutes before, I'd tucked my son into bed on a Friday night. I was enjoying a drink with my wife. It was a particularly good night, and we both felt young, with a weekend ahead of us that hadn't been spoken for. It would be a weekend with my wife and son. Given how much I'd missed of their lives by being deployed, this was no small thing.

But I answered the phone. An unanswered call could cost me my career. The real reason I grabbed the phone is that I'd trained hard to make it to the big leagues, to the Special Forces, and the distinct honor of having my country call on me and my team to do things few in the world could pull off was no small thing to me. I'd fought through sweat and blood to be part of this elite A-Team, and I lived by its creed and culture of success.

When I picked up the phone, I heard a voice I know well. It was Paul, my team sergeant. His voice was a little different than usual, but he gave no indication why I was being called in at this time of night. It was just a routine, "Stube, this is Paul. You need to come on in to the team room."

With that, it was understood that I didn't have time to pass Go or to collect $200. I just had to get straight to the team room within 30 minutes.

Paul was never one to emphasize anything too much. He was a firm believer in "big boy rules." He always gave everyone enough rope to let soldiers hang themselves, which is great if you hate micromanagers, but bad if you tend to bend the rules. Either way, Paul expected the best of everyone; if you'd been told it was a 30-minute response time to get to the unit after a call, he wouldn't repeat this to you. Paul was very personable and fun, but he knew where to draw the line at mission time.

With my maturity somewhat lacking, my transition between joking and seriousness was often slower than it should have been. Paul didn't have this problem. Paul absolutely loved the television show *The Simpsons,* and he loved hockey. His conversations about those two things were often so animated and passionate that it would shock me how he could turn it off so quickly without the lingering hint of a smile. But Paul had been around longer than I had. He knew that it's better to get serious on your own than for situations to turn ugly and dictate a new attitude for you. He was the team sergeant for good reason. I recall him always showing empathy and understanding, but that he was completely uncompromising regarding policies and standards. I enjoyed his hybrid sort of leadership; it was usually one or the other. With Paul, you knew he hadn't forgotten where he had come from, and that he expected the highest standards.

I left the house, having said goodbyes in the most appropriate way I could. It had to be a significant goodbye, in case it became a lengthy trip, or worse. But I never wanted to go overboard with this, as it could scare my wife and, anyway, I might be back home soon. Now I feel differently. If I could go back in time, I would go way overboard to express my love every time, as you just don't know. If nothing else, it serves as a good excuse to communicate things we may otherwise be failing at with our loved ones.

After I left my family, and as I drove fast to meet the team, I inevitably thought, *Now what the hell am I doing this for?*

Saying goodbye to your family with the chance that it's forever makes you reflect on your decision to answer this call. Whatever you do for a living, the call to lead will force you to take self-inventory and to continuously re-evaluate or justify your own commitment. When it costs you something, you find how strong your beliefs really are. Yes. There it is again. For better or for worse, the call to lead has a lot rolled into it.

You find that sacrifice doesn't begin and end with a soldier responding to a call that could result in his or her death. Each one of us who leaves family on a business trip, or who goes in to work early or stays late, is, in a way, making this same decision. Balancing work and our private lives is never easy, but clarity comes when we clearly see why we're going on any mission. That clarity comes from action.

As I drove, I asked myself, *Is it a genetic trait, a learned or cultural underpinning, or the result of a singular experience in my life? What makes us decide to answer the call—even, in a way, to crave it?*

When I made it past the guard post and to the team room, I found some of my teammates were already there. Steve had the farthest to drive, but he was always the first one there and, as usual, had the least to say. Dan showed the salt of experience, but always shared everything he knew with all of us, having spontaneous mini-training sessions at every opportunity. Now he had a look of acceptance and resolve as if to say, "Well, boys, training time is over. Time to put it to work!" JC was there with an excited, boyish grin. He always got that eager, if not mischievous, look when it came time for something dangerous or unknown. He kept playfully saying, "Uh-oh...uh-oh...." Of course, Paul was there, and he simply had an unreadable poker face that came with the job of herding kitty cats, or an assortment of alpha male Green Berets, which is a similar challenge.

On this particular night, there was no indication of why the team had been called in. There wasn't a hint or clue until all eleven of us were there. I noticed each person had a clear difference in his attitude and response to the situation. One person was not at peace with the timing of this, as if there was unfinished business at home. I saw anxiety on the faces of some, while others were stoic. There was a cheerleader in the room; he was the type who throws out motivational comments and pats others on the back or offers encouraging handshakes. We weren't yet a team; we weren't yet all a part of a shared experience, as everyone had yet to arrive and our mission had not yet been presented to us.

This felt like the minutes in a corporate boardroom before the boss gets there with the big news. If the boss is smart, he or she will pull the team together behind the news on an active mission to make something measurable happen. If he or she doesn't do this, they risk dividing the team and causing it to split into many unhappy parts. Morale falls when this happens. Dissension begins.

In the Special Forces, and without fail in these environments, there are one or two more aggressive, if not primitive, types. These guys are invariably chomping at the bit and salivating at the possibility of shooting bad guys. That's a different reality than most are used to. To be state-sponsored agents for killing is a different role, which dictates quite a different mindset than any other career field. This advanced warrior mindset isn't for everyone. One of the most interesting things in this community is the range of personalities that successfully negotiate the daily realities of killing and dying. The characteristics men employ to deal with it can be a part of them seemingly from birth, or they might be developed traits. Some appear to maintain a complete persona that just fits—it seems to be them. Others apply measures of compensation while they maintain a more "normal" personality.

Though lives might not be at risk when a corporate team meets and gets a call to action, these same emotions are at play. Pulling the different parts together and pointing them toward a goal is what a leader must do.

Soon the whole Green Beret A-Team was present. We were all eager to move to the next step, whatever it might be. We knew something official was taking place, as there was a representative among us whom none of us knew. He appeared to have been introduced to the Team

Sergeant and Commander before we arrived, and we could only speculate on where he was from or which agency he represented.

At this point, the entire team was being ushered to a nearby isolation facility. Any isolation facility must completely restrict communications and passage in and out of it. Personnel and information must be completely managed and controlled from a security standpoint to maintain the clandestine nature of what must be performed. Once gathered under guard at an isolation facility, everyone is waiting for an important representative of National Defense to arrive with a high-level commander. No two of these are exactly alike, but they happen the same way. At this point, the biggest question in everyone's mind is whether this is a training event or a real-world mission. If it is only a training mission, the tricky part is that it may not be revealed to the team until some point well into, or even after, the planning phase. You may not know it's a training mission until you're on an airplane with the mindset that "this is for all the marbles." There is no shortage of pucker factor in any of these situations.

An initial briefing outlines what the situation is in a particular area of interest. It will then be steered into the fine point where a specific mission could help or solve a given situation or crisis or achieve a stated objective. Higher authorities will have already conducted a screening and selection process so the right team is chosen to perform the mission. Sometimes two, or even three, teams will be isolated in order to take the selection process even further. Depending on the priority or visibility of the mission, these multiple teams will go through the planning process for an ultimate selection based on the merits of each plan, rehearsals, and overall readiness for the task at hand.

Competition for the best missions remains on our minds throughout our time on the A-Team. If only one team is going, I want it to be mine. Some corporations employ these strategies by having several teams compete to create the best products or plans for launching a new product. This can be very effective, if done correctly.

These missions remain the ultimate culmination of training and performance, as well as a validation for that training and performance. To be the best of the best is the objective, and selection for these missions represents just that.

So we'd been selected to participate in the process, if not perform the mission. Now began one of the things that makes a Special Forces' team absolutely unique to the military. The members of the team actually develop and write the plan for any mission they conduct as a team. Anywhere else in the military, mission plans are developed and handed down *to* the team, or developed by the immediate command. In the Green Berets, you are not handed a mission plan and simply told to follow its steps. Who would write such a thing? Someone at their desk in the State Department? Someone who has never been in our boots behind enemy lines? No. A Green Beret A-Team has been trained physically and mentally to write and execute missions. What we are given are constraints, restraints, and available military intelligence to develop the mission according to *our* strengths and weaknesses.

Empowering a team this way leads to unexpected solutions and tends to bring the best out in people. They become a part of the mission, not just a pawn. This unleashes greatness. More businesses need to find ways to empower their teams, to empower the people who know their jobs best, and encourage them to write mission plans they will ultimately execute themselves.

In the case of a Green Beret A-Team, each unique skill set possessed by the members of the team is used to contribute critical planning elements. The members on the team are the subject-matter experts best suited to creating successful methods and plans to accomplish any mission. Within the Army Special Forces A-Teams, respective skill areas include the medic, engineer, weapons, tactics specialist, and communications.

As the planning phase began, personalities and creativity came to light, as they always do. This is where teamwork takes on a unique role. As the plan took shape, it presented unique challenges that had to be answered—potentially, lives were at stake.

As vulnerabilities and complexities were revealed or created by the plan, it put further demands on separate parts of the plan. Because each member is assigned a specific part to complete, one may find himself having to change all or part of the plan to accommodate an accepted idea presented in another facet of the plan. It may also be unique that a role requiring physical performance also needs academic work.

After two or three days of planning, discussion, and course of action development, we all began wishing we could see our loved ones. The perilous nature of some of the mission planning made this feeling more profound. The perilous nature of the mission forces thoughts of mortality, of the possibility of not seeing our loved ones again. But, now, it's on to rehearsals. The plan has been presented and approved, and it's time to practice. Rehearsals are the single greatest tool for eliminating unforeseen failures in any plan, but most corporations don't rehearse at all. Even if folks rehearse plans, they often don't leave themselves enough time to do so adequately. In the Special Forces, we must forget about home and family—we really don't even talk about that. We are trained to forget about personal issues. Mission first! At this point, it is mission only.

Again, this is one of those moments that forces you to question your own convictions. You *must* question your own decision to answer the call now, because the performance of these duties foregoes everything you love about your personal life and family—even your own freedom. This is when I would occasionally wonder if maybe I should have stayed in Tennessee with some of my friends from high school. It was easy to imagine everything back home as fun and easygoing. It was easy to picture my friends working the farm and living the good country life. The more I thought of the beauty of apple pie and baseball in American life, the more I found myself growing more resolute in my commitment to serve and defend. Indeed, I rediscovered the beauty of freedom itself as I pondered what else I could be doing as an American. My question was answered. My commitment was still valid, after all. I would often recall friends back home saying they wished they had joined the military when I did. But, given how much they were doing for our society in different ways, for me it felt tragic to think of them being in the military. I really love the idea of each person doing what they are most compelled to do. It ensures that America will continue to be great and do great things if each person does what they prefer and are naturally driven to be the best at. I didn't have a farm or family business to step into. My professional aspirations were in national defense. Everything fit. I was where I was supposed to be. Considering my family in this decision, I truly wanted them to remain free and safe. This consistently begged the question, "If not me, then who?" Once again, my mission focus intensified and I soldiered on. Time to put my selfish concerns aside and lean forward in the foxhole once again.

When the mission preparation concludes, you may be only a couple miles from home, but you can't risk the mission by going home to kiss your wife. Instead, you board an aircraft that will take you far away for an unspecified amount of time. It will likely deliver you to conditions that have previously claimed the lives of peers and friends, and will hold the potential to claim yours.

While you may believe you're prepared to die, and you may very well be killed, it seems more difficult to prepare for disabling wounds and the conditions that might follow—changing your life forever. That's the stuff you have to hang around and deal with in a worldly sense. This comes down to service beyond sacrifice. The consequences may be less significant in other roles, but answering the call is no less consuming if you take your life goals seriously.

The consequences may not be your own to bear. If others pay a price for decisions we make, it puts measurable consequence on us, as well. I saw in my own commander a painful reality in dealing with the effects on others, whether directly or indirectly, caused by his decisions. It obviously hurt him to deal with what my injuries did to my life, career, and family. His suffering may never subside due to loss of life under his command in combat, though we all know it's just a reality that comes with the territory.

In the business world, this also applies. If an employee is staying late to finish a project, or taking that extra business trip, then they are also sacrificing home life for their vocation and goals. A leader needs to make sure his or her employees aren't just rewarded for this; they also must make certain this individual effort is necessary. Did the team fail this person and, therefore, are they being left to do what the team should? Is this person so driven they are in danger of burnout? Is the workplace so disorganized that goals can't be met during normal business hours? Is the team in need of more support? All of these questions should be answered by team members and leadership as you run through practice sessions, and as you push forward toward mission goals later.

This is just some of what each of us must deal with if we are to lead. Somewhere at the beginning, when we sought this role, we decided to respond to the call to lead. At the basis of all of this must be a profound answer to why we are sacrificing for this goal. If there isn't a deep reason, we are likely to lose our way and fail.

At this beginning stage, we might also decide that a particular mission in life is not for us—there is nothing wrong with that. If we decide it *is* for us, go in with eyes as wide open as possible. This means seeking out mentors and asking them what the role we're interested in is really like, what it really requires of us. If you want to be a salesperson, you should consider what the responsibilities, sacrifices, and more are for the head salesperson. That is who you are following and where you are headed. Really try to understand, in human terms, what that role requires to decide if it is really for you.

In the Green Berets, almost every mission starts with a phone call at night. As I said, you have a certain amount of time to get to the team room. You will then go to an isolation facility. Once everyone on the team is there, no one goes in or out except for one person. An entourage from command gives you an objective. They give you your constraints and restraints. You have 72 hours to plan a mission to achieve the goal within those constraints and restraints. You can request information, but you don't have phones or internet access. You might think life and business are more complex than these intense calls to action, but they are not. Green Beret missions might be a more compressed series of actions, but the same fundamental rules apply.

This is why they are a great example for showing all of us how to deal with high-stress situations to create plans to achieve our goals. I spent four years as a cadre in the distinguished John F. Kennedy Special Warfare Center and School at Fort Bragg, teaching men to be Green Berets. The Special Forces way is especially relevant in these times where political expediency too often rules. I taught my students at the Warfare Center that it's voluntarily bipolar to think you can be one person at work and another at home. You have to be a leader all the time. The military enforces this. To be effective, the academic and business communities need to do the same, as well. So, before you leap into a role, you must do your best to understand clearly the role and to decide whether it is really for you. Unless you are completely committed to the role, you will fail or be mediocre.

Corporations also must do a better job at explaining these things to people they are interviewing and potentially hiring. People will naturally try to sell themselves to anyone interviewing them, even if they know in their gut that the job isn't for them. The Special Forces employ many physical and mental tests with the cadre members watching closely for doubts and weaknesses. This is effective to cut the recruit pool down continuously in order to find those who might best fit the all-consuming role of a Green Beret. In fact, throughout the tenure of a candidate or qualified Green Beret, it is abundantly clear that assessment never stops. This doesn't mean that those who fail aren't worthy. Actually, many who fail simply had the misfortune of getting injured or sick at the wrong time. But, really, what it means is that this isn't the role for them. They are meant to do something else, maybe even something that's more important.

If they are really meant to play this role, to grow into a Green Beret or something else, then the next steps in forging a leader are designed to make them prove it to their bosses and to themselves.

From the pop-music icon Billy Ocean to personal and professional mentors, we hear these words from time to time: "When the going gets tough, the tough get going." However, it may not be about being "tough" at all. The longer we live to see situations unfold, it becomes clearer that either we control a situation or the situation controls us. With this in mind, it becomes a smart choice more than a tough one to get out in front of a problem. We can still call on that mental toughness, but I think it's just smart. Those of us who wish to be in front of a problem, influencing positive outcomes, rather than dealing with less fortunate ones handed to us later, are, to a degree, called to lead.

Of course, defining leadership and analyzing how it is done seems to be a popular thing. I see a great deal produced by academic think tanks, where true leadership is treated, well, academically. To them, a collection of traits and competencies are agreed upon and listed in bulleted lists on PowerPoint slides. While I understand leadership must be personified in order to really be understood and communicated, I can't help but feel that leadership is something different in each person.

What I mean is that leadership is a very personal thing, and it is personality driven.

Also, most people I know just aren't great at memorizing from slide shows. I've found that in the field, following a critical incident, most bullet points wind up uselessly scattered on the ground. In my experience, the "experts" are too often people who haven't learned practical things by fire. They have textbook experience, and maybe even an idea that feels good, but not real-world experience.

No, this isn't some trodden down, anti-intellectual, blue-collar inferiority complex talking. It's more of a feeling that some things just can't be cerebrally managed without being coupled with real world experience—and I mean worst-case experience, not best case. I've even known people with very little experience in life who decided to start reading heavily and talking to others in order to become leadership experts so they can write books to save mankind. I suppose we are to be thankful. Most often, I presume, it is a way to make money. Either way, it proves that there is often a void where leadership should be, and that anyone willing to stand in front can garner attention and even resources, at least, for a short time.

Still, because a person is loud and authoritative doesn't mean that the person knows what they are talking about or that they are dependable and trustworthy. In the real world, some of the most basic rules for a leader are broken consistently, and even constantly. It starts with not using a leadership position to leverage profit, personal gain, or pleasure. It continues with never putting yourself in a position where you take from your subordinates in any way—you must build up your team, not kill initiative by stealing from them.

Real leaders finish last. By this, I mean they are last to eat, last to take time off, and last to gain in any way from the work being done. It's about empowering your people with everything possible to achieve success. It's about knowing that, as the leader, you are not the functional element of the team. For the best odds of success, you need to serve your team as a leader.

The type of leader we are will often dictate the length of our leadership position. If we command any authority at all, it is different than having it officially assigned, and it comes from a short list of traits.

Some are learned, and some, possibly, we are born with. These are listed in a number of ways, but simply put, our authority is legal, cultural, practical, or charismatic. Regardless of how we wind up in the role of a leader, we should approach it humbly, with the same sense of responsibility for the outcome and for the team. Always remember that we can freely delegate authority within the scope of our leadership, but that we can absolutely never delegate the responsibility that is ours alone as the leader.

I've witnessed the call to lead taking place. I've seen the call answered by simply who a person is. I've also seen people forged like a hammer into leaders, with painful mistakes and consequences serving as a compass for all they do now. For them, the call may come differently, but it comes. It is important to be mindful that failure is possible, particularly when we think we are above it, or when we think too highly of ourselves.

The whole leadership thing started very early for me. Well, not being a leader, but hearing all about what leadership is. As a military brat, I heard the words used frequently. At that time, I defined it in my mind that the leader was the boss. Now, I know that leaders aren't necessarily the boss, and the boss isn't necessarily a leader—not fun facts, at times, but true nevertheless.

To be the leader we really want to be, we must select a code to follow at all times. A triad of moral, ethical, and legal standards must be decided upon and lived up to, both at home and at work. To decide consciously to be two different people at work versus elsewhere is to be, as I mentioned, voluntarily bipolar.

We are often told to "Know thyself." The problem is that we aren't always what we want to be, or ought to be, or even what we *think* we are. So that's really a call to decide who we want to be, and then initiating the action necessary to make it so. Then we need to be that person, with that code, *all the time*. We have the right to be anything we want to at any time, but we can also effectively disqualify ourselves from any legitimate leadership role or identity in the process. Will those you lead answer the call if you don't? Are you the kind of person someone will follow, even if they must sacrifice or face risk to do it? It's about having a moral code that will help shape your personal and professional identity.

Answering the call has its drawbacks. That's why we must decide who we are, and what we believe in. The day comes when we are tested, and our commitment comes into question. Not by anyone else, but by us. We will have to re-address our decisions to serve. No matter how seemingly beautiful and redeeming that service may be or appear to others, we will be tested and have to answer to ourselves. Why am I doing this? Is it worth it? I've heard it said that our commitment to ideals becomes clearer when we stand to lose something in order to remain in support of them.

Very early on in life, those questions came most often in direct proportion to how hard the work was, how bad the food was, and how long I was away from home. Simple comforts drove the train for me as a child. Then came the Army.

I still clearly remember the drill sergeant who all but dragged "my carcass" off the bus as I clung to all I possessed in two duffel bags. This was different. Everything was hard and worn around me. Nothing was comfortable. No one was kind, or even wanted to be. I asked myself, *How could anyone live like this?* I wasn't asked nicely or encouraged to do anything at all. There were only overly dramatic and painful consequences for my failure to comply with even minute details of how I was ordered to conduct myself. From personal hygiene to how I wore the clothing I was issued, everything had a prescribed method to it. Everything.

I asked myself why I had volunteered for this. I repeatedly asked myself if it was worth it. Sometimes I wondered if I should try to change my life goals and look for a way out. Each time, I came to the same sort of answer. I had to keep something bigger than myself in focus. I had been tied to what I considered patriotic convictions from a very young age, but this was the first time I ever had to sacrifice or suffer to hold onto them. My commitment was being tested. It would happen again many more times in serious ways so that the experiences would make me feel silly about this one.

Answering the call would bring on progressively more serious tests of my commitment. Some of it is very obvious as part of being in the military while conflict occurs worldwide. But the call may get answered in ways less obvious, lesser known, and seldom witnessed by the citizenry of our nation. As a cultural difference in my life, I had to realize that, in the military, I was fully allowed to have a personal life, but I may not be given much time or latitude to enjoy it. It is a change in life to surrender personal choice and liberties. It's difficult when there's no limit to it, because your accountability applies 24 hours a day, seven days a week. Your personal life becomes, well, your personal life. If the Army didn't issue it to you, then it is not their concern, and it's best if non-Army issues never arise. Mandatory breaks from all personal life and details can last days, weeks, months, and even years, in the military. Those costs can never be measured in the scope of a life.

To be certain, the enemy doesn't take days off or observe holidays, so, as a warrior, I missed a pretty big collection of them, which I can never get back or make up.

Through it all, I had to remain in a posture to answer the call because of who I'd decided to be, who I wanted to be. This seemed particularly true after all the rungs had been met through the arduous process of Special Forces training in general and, particularly, as a medical sergeant. The training was tough, and it seemingly lasted forever, but then came the uncertainty of mysterious missions and danger. This is where you learn that your life is an acceptable loss in the pursuit of national objectives. These clandestine missions have a process to them that I will never forget. Being ready for them requires that answering the call be shifted from an occasional concern to a permanent way of life.

Everything about answering the call to lead here might be a little more extreme than the corporate world is used to, as in the Special Forces, you are literally putting your life on the line. Many, many of my Green Beret brothers—men I served with and men I trained—have died in the service of this great country. But with that said, someone entering any career faces stresses and sacrifices. They might not be putting their life on the line—though, if they are a police officer or a firefighter, for example, they are—but they're giving up things in order to achieve things, in order to learn to lead, and then to lead.

This decision is a critical step in becoming all we want to be. Next comes understanding your role in the context of all of those who support you.

4

DON'T NEGLECT YOUR SUPPORT NETWORK

If All You Do Is Look Up You Won't See All Those Holding You Up

"It's amazing what you can accomplish if you don't care who gets the credit."

—HARRY S. TRUMAN

Though a Green Beret A-Team is a part of the tip of the U.S. Army's spear, they are only one part of it. Without all of the people behind them, they wouldn't be anything but well-trained, Type A badasses wishing they could get into the fight. And I guess, on some level, I knew that without air support and the pilots resupplying us with pallets of ammo, and so many others supporting us, we wouldn't have had a chance of completing a mission. But when I was on an A-Team, I didn't think all that much about the supporting roles holding me up.

Still, there were powerful reminders.

At one point during a mission, we had to intentionally blow up two of our own vehicles out in the soft sand of the Red Desert. We were deep in Taliban country and the vehicles were done. Command lost it when we did this. Sure, a vehicle failure in a combat environment can get you killed if you try to stay with the thing. You can't wait on the Army's version of AAA roadside assistance. When a Humvee or other vehicle breaks down or gets stuck, you either have to get it running or remove all sensitive items from it by cross-loading the gear to other vehicles. Then you have to destroy the broken vehicle by blowing it up—you just can't leave it for the enemy to make use of. But when you blow up two vehicles, one after the other, command starts telling you combat vehicles are in short supply and that, if you keep doing that, you just might have to be evacuated out. We were being sent in to cut off the escape routes of Taliban fighters while a large force of Canadian and other soldiers pushed in from the north. This was a planned mission. Without us in place, the Taliban could just slip away to fight another day.

So they sent us a mechanic, a man whose back was bent by a very heavy toolbox he carried as he walked down the ramp of a loud and powerful CH-47 Chinook helicopter and into the heavy, swirling dust. His job was to hit the ground with our Special Forces operation to fix everything he could before being evacuated hours later.

But then, the big battle described in Chapter 1 started, and he was stuck with us for much longer than he'd imagined. As in any company, in the U.S. Army, about nine out of 10 people are in support of the troops on the front lines, and he didn't expect to be thrust into the 10 percent who look through gun sights at the enemy.

That mechanic, who hadn't fired his weapon much since Basic, was white-knuckled, gripping his M4 carbine as he returned fire. At first, he told anyone who would listen that he didn't belong there. No one gave him a hard time about this. No one even laughed or shook their head. Green Berets in the throes of battle don't have time for that macho nonsense. They just showed him how it's done and he responded by manning up to the fight.

Then another reminder of the need for our support network shook us. As we fought, we almost ran out of ammo. We had to pull back several times to receive airdropped pallets of ammunition. I found out later that men and women back at base were working double-shifts and waking up in the middle of the night just to pack pallets of ammo for us. Without them, we'd have been dead.

Though our need for our support network was life or death in this case, any business will also struggle and maybe die if its support network—its parts supply chain, subcontractors, and more—fails them. In business, this means finding contractors and subcontractors and the men and women in other businesses you might buy from or sell to that you can trust. The old saying "You never know who you can count on until you're down" is true, but there is a savvy method for vetting people before a crisis strikes that I tried to teach aspiring soldiers.

Before getting to that, I should clarify that I am not speaking about the U.S. Army in general, here, but about a Green Beret A-Team. The Army can be a very bureaucratic, and even politically correct, institution. An army's purpose is to fight and win wars, but, today, the U.S. Military is tasked with much more than simply defeating an enemy on the battlefield. Of course, that central purpose alone should keep their mission and purpose clear, but it often doesn't. The U.S. Armed Forces have very political responsibilities, and a deep, and often intractable, bureaucracy. This makes the Army, in general, more like a large corporation. Its size and the fear of bad public relations, and even of accountability for a failed mission, can make it lose its way.

Let me give you an example from my co-author.

One bright August morning in 2011, he walked past the White House, past that gallant statue of Andrew Jackson up on his horse with his hat in his hand in Lafayette Park, and then went into the headquarters of the U.S. Chamber of Commerce in Washington, D.C. He was doing research for a book on how we can save what's left of the U.S. Bill of Rights, and he had a doozy of a question for R. Bruce Josten, who was then the second ranking officer at the U.S. Chamber of Commerce.

The Chamber represents more than three million businesses. Yet none of these millions of businesses had legally challenged the campaign-finance restrictions that had muzzled their speech near elections. It took a small, independent nonprofit named Citizens United to purposely make a film critical of Hillary Clinton, a film they knew would be censored during the 2008 election process, in order to force the courts to question the constitutionality of preventing corporations, associations, and more, from engaging in the political process near elections.

When Josten was asked why none of those millions of companies had the gumption to fight for their rights, he said, "Businesses have stock holders and bottom lines. They're not going to take strong political positions like that."

From his big, bright office with windows overlooking Washington, D.C.'s Capitol Hill, he explained that companies rise and fall on their reputations. This often makes them careful, plotting, even overly cautious. They aren't like politicians. They can't be affiliated with a party, an ideology. They must be affiliated with everyone who might buy their products. So they want to be seen for what they create, not what their owners and leadership think.

He said, "They task us with fights like that." But even the Chamber didn't have the gumption or clarity to tackle that particular fight. The Chamber did submit friend-of-the-court briefs in favor of overturning the First Amendment restrictions in question in the Citizen's United case, however.

Josten had a point. Businesses, big or small, are a very poor check on government overreach or largesse. Actually, bigger companies are the ones that can afford lobbyists to defend themselves, while the smaller ones can't even do that. So the business community might offer a little resistance to the power of government, but they are unlikely to force a showdown with government officials over a constitutional right. They might use lobbyists to do this for them—and. thereby, to shield them from public attacks—but they are more likely simply to look to carve out exemptions and loopholes so they can prosper in the changing system.

There are incredible exceptions, but you have to search for these, as great companies, like great individuals, often don't want to tell their story about standing up for their rights. They want to be known for what they make, not what they think. Such was the stance of a little American company named Magpul, a company founded with ideals formed in the U.S. Military.

Richard Fitzpatrick, Magpul's founder and CEO, was serving with Alpha Company, 3rd Recon Battalion in the U.S. Marine Corps in 1991 when he first started thinking about inventing a rubberized loop to replace the paracord-and-duct-tape loops that had long been a standard part of many SOPs (Standard Operating Procedures) in the military, dating back to Vietnam. He was one of the soldiers who used duct tape and paracord to make loops that they'd attach to the bases of rifle magazines. These loops would help them locate the magazines from ammo pouches and to control them, even in the dark, as they turned them 180 degrees and inserted them into a rifle.

In the late 1980s, the standard-issue "ALICE" magazine pouches tended to be oversized and swallow up all but the top half-inch of the magazine. This made paracord loops essential so a soldier could get a grip on the magazine when under stress.

Fitzpatrick first tried gluing pieces of rubber tubing together to make a prototype, but they didn't work well enough to suit him. Still, the idea kept turning over in his mind. Years later, in 1997, after he had been out of the Marine Corps for a few years, a solution occurred to him. He decided to try a dual-friction band. He played with the idea in his garage in Colorado. It worked. He patented the idea and used his savings to pay for a small injection mold so he could manufacture parts in Erie, Colorado.

This original mold was built from a simple drawing. Fitzpatrick didn't have the money to pay for engineering changes if the final part for the mold was incorrect—yeah, all of his money was on the table. Luckily, the first samples came back perfect—so perfect, that when the mold was finally replaced a decade later, no adjustments had to be made from the original.

Fitzpatrick named the loop the "Magpul" for "MAGazine PULL." At the time, his intention was simply to make a series of Magpul loops in different calibers. He first introduced the product at the 1999 NDIA (National Defense Institute Association) Small Arms Symposium in Parsippany, New Jersey. He says it was met with a lot of interest but no orders. While Magpul initially focused on a military contract, many of its first sales were from discretionary unit purchases within the branches of the U.S. Military, individual sales via its website, and through dealer sales at trade shows. Bureaucracies move slowly, but those who shoot in competitions, and some in the military, were finding Magpul was a solution they needed.

The real growth of the company would come when they focused on education rather than direct advertising. "A classic example of this was a 24-page booklet titled 'Advanced Tactical Reloading' we included with every package of Magpuls we sold," said Fitzpatrick. "It had over 60 illustrations in it and was very detailed. Because of this detail, users became experts on the product and went on to become ambassadors for Magpul."

Though they didn't foresee some of their products being made illegal for sale by the state of Colorado, as Magpul grew, Fitzpatrick decided they needed a creed to keep their mission clear and their identity founded on sound principles, just as he had as a U.S. Marine. To do this, Fitzpatrick began creating what he calls Magpul's "Foundations." They are a series of principles based on action. They outline a creative and critical way of thinking that would benefit anyone looking to start a business or simply trying to get a company back on track. Its Foundations started as a series of quotes they used to stay focused as the company grew. "In 2007, during a website redesign," said Fitzpatrick, "we added the Ayn Rand quotes, along with an explanation why each quote matters to Magpul, and then published it as the guiding philosophy behind the company."

Some of the quotes have been a little controversial, such as, "Build what they need, not what they want." Fitzpatrick explained that people often can't articulate what they really want, but that if you listen and think critically, you can develop what they really need.

In a section of Magpul's Foundations titled "Annoy the Establishment," Magpul says, "Just as America's Founding Fathers sought to promote individual rights and freedoms over those of the collective, Magpul also stands on the side of the individual. The natural enemy of the individual and innovation is the establishment and bureaucracy (which literally means 'the power of the desk'). When we are annoying the establishment, we know we are effectively upholding our principles." This is not to be confused with radical demonstrations and protest, seen all too often.

According to Magpul's leadership, those in government procurement have quoted the "annoy the establishment" line back to them more than once, but that's fine with them. Their view is if they make a solid product, it will sell.

In another part of its creed, in a section under the subhead "Profits Are Not Evil," they say, "Magpul's view on profits (and money, in general) is summed up in the following quote by Ayn Rand: 'Money is the material shape of the principle that men who wish to deal with one another must deal by trade and give value for value.'" This quote is from Rand's book *Atlas Shrugged*—published in 1957, the novel depicts a dystopian United States, wherein leading industrialists begin vanishing from society in response to oppressive regulations. The industrial leaders in the novel go to a secret society based on honest commerce that's free from the bureaucrats who feed off the hard work of others. Rand placed the secret society in Colorado's mountains.

Fitzpatrick said, "The irony in *Atlas Shrugged* where the railroad employee said, 'We can't lose Colorado. It's our last hope,' was not lost on us. We're openly pro *laissez-faire* capitalism, individual rights, and personal responsibility. Outside of that, we purposely stay out of individual political commentary or political endorsements, as that is not our area of expertise."

The last part of its Foundations covers what Magpul calls an "Unfair Advantage." Fitzpatrick says this is an abbreviation of the old military saying: "If you show up for a fair fight, you are unprepared." He says this is a nod to the general U.S. Marine recon culture.

Obviously, someone with this clear of a vision isn't going to stand for his products being banned for ideological reasons.

In December 2012, Magpul Industries was preparing to break ground on a new state-of-the-art facility in Colorado. Magpul's PMAG magazines, AR stocks, grips, and other products were in high demand. Magpul had, by then, grown to be more than 200 employees, and the future looked bright. But then the state's Democratic-led legislature and its governor, John Hickenlooper, decided the way to stop sociopaths from taking advantage of "gun-free zones" is to restrict law-abiding citizens' freedom. At the time, Colorado's Senate President, John Morse, stood on the Senate floor and argued that new gun restrictions were needed as a way of "cleansing a sickness from our souls."

Fitzpatrick said, "The magnitude of what was being proposed forced us into the political arena almost immediately. We had an economic defense that could be mounted against the bill, whereas the arguments that should have held more weight—those of liberty—were being ignored by those in power. That said, the decision to uproot and leave Colorado was not made lightly. There were a lot of conversations internally about this, and a lot of sleepless nights, but, in the end, we all agreed that holding true to our principles was the only thing that felt right, whatever the outcome or threat to the business."

Magpul, and other companies in the state, responded to the emotionally charged, anti-gun rhetoric by saying they'd be forced to take their jobs out of Colorado if the state banned the sale of some of their products. A lot of freedom-loving Coloradoans also protested the proposed gun-control legislation. Many also pointed out that all the facts show the proposed Second Amendment infringements wouldn't stop the bad guys with guns, but, if anything, would only enable them. Almost all of the state's sheriffs also came out against the ban.

The legislature and governor, however, went ahead and banned so-called "high-capacity" magazines (in this case, those holding more than 15 rounds), required "universal background checks," and much more.

After the ban passed, but before it went into effect, Magpul instituted what it called "the Boulder Airlift." Named after the post-World War II Berlin Airlift, the Boulder Airlift was a massive effort to produce and distribute as many so-called "high-capacity" magazines as it could before they were made illegal for sale.

Then, after the magazine ban went into effect, Magpul made good on its word. After a detailed search for new locations, they announced that Magpul was "moving operations to states that support our culture of individual liberties and personal responsibility." He then explained that Magpul was relocating manufacturing, distribution, and shipping operations to Cheyenne, Wyoming. Magpul's corporate office was moved to Texas. Texas's then-governor Rick Perry gave Magpul a big Texas welcome. In a statement, Perry said, "In Texas, we understand that freedom breeds prosperity, which is why we've built our economy around principles that allow employers to innovate, keep more of what they earn, and create jobs."

Magpul, however, retained a limited presence in Colorado. Duane Liptak, Director, Product Management and Marketing for Magpul, said, "Magpul is committed to maintaining an operation in Colorado to ensure the company is supporting lawful gun owners in our native state."

There is a moral to the story about Magpul. Without its steadfast adherence to its core principles, Magpul would have alienated much of its customer base and shattered its innovative philosophy. After all, if it had given in, its first thought wouldn't have been its customers' needs, but, instead, *Will the bureaucrats give this idea their approval?* That's a European way of thinking, not American.

To this end, Fitzpatrick said, "At first glance, some people do not realize that Magpul is first and foremost a design and engineering company. Our product development structure is rather unique, because it blends end-users with a great deal of experience (Magpul CORE) with innovative industrial designers and a formidable staff of engineers. This results in many disciplines, all interacting in a creative atmosphere that is best described as inspirational, with a healthy dose of checks and balances to keep things real.

"Even as we innovate, we place a great deal of emphasis on customer service," said Fitzpatrick. "We keep things in-house so that when you do need technical advice or support, it's coming from someone who is very familiar with our products and the way that they work. We also spend a lot of time on various social media outlets and forums, and this includes everyone from customer service to the CEO. We like to be able to answer questions in a setting that allows others to find the information."

Now, with all this said, it's worth noting that a man's (or a company's) character isn't really known until tested. Rudyard Kipling put this maxim into poetry with "If." ("If you can keep your head when all about you; Are losing theirs and blaming it on you...you'll be a Man, my son!") So Magpul was tested, and, like some other notable gun and gun-related manufacturers, it stood up for its principles and for us.

But Magpul wouldn't have done so well under fire if it hadn't developed such a clear definition of its mission and of itself before one of its major products was banned by its home state. Fitzpatrick learned this in the military. He also learned how to bring his support network into his team. Like almost every manufacturer, Magpul buys and receives parts from a lot of subcontractors. These subcontractors also came under political pressure when Magpul's fight began with the state of Colorado. Fitzpatrick says it was his team identity and the relationships he had built on that basis that saw him through a fight to survive that very easily could have killed his relatively new business.

In the Green Berets, we run practice missions with our support network involved in order to test the strengths and weaknesses not just of our team, but also of our support networks. Can they get us the gear we need on time? If things go bad, can we count on a support network to get us out fast? Sometimes, when we found weaknesses before a mission in our support network, we actually brought in experts to teach us how to hotwire specific types of vehicles or to do other things. We needed to know the strengths and weaknesses of our support network in order to prepare for these kinds of potential problems.

To keep it going after the practice sessions takes real, openhearted honesty. I saw this many times during missions in the Green Berets. Magpul even had a moment where they could have pointed fingers and thereby shirked responsibility and harmed their support network. Like men and women, now and then, companies, even the best, mess up. How they handle a mistake says a lot about them. Magpul had such an issue. A production mold error with its Glock PMAG 17 GL9s was causing failures. Magpul immediately mailed replacements to every customer who purchased one of these magazines. They also fixed the problem—the magazines are now all working. Here's how they handled the issue on their Facebook page:

> OK we screwed up.
>
> After initial release of the Glock PMAG 17 GL9 a few days ago we started seeing random issues of failure to feed with the new magazine in other Glock models, primarily the Glock 19 and 26. Of all the challenges of building a Glock magazine with a single new composite, issues like drop free, impact strength and feed lip retention were foremost on our mind. The failure to feed came as a bit of a surprise to us and we immediately headed out to the range to investigate.
>
> In short order we found the problem. Without getting into technical details, some small, but critical geometry changes did not make it into the initial production molds. We should have caught this but no failures showed up on our factory guns during live fire testing and flaws in our internal processes of checks/balances did not flag the oversight as it should.

So as I said before, we screwed up and here is what we are going to do about it.

Molds are being updated with the correct geometry as we speak and a replacement magazine body with the correct geometry should be available by May 4th, 2015....

–Richard Fitzpatrick, President/CEO Magpul Industries Corp

If Fitzpatrick instead blamed a supplier, an overseas manufacturer making parts of Magpul, or another part of his support network, then he would have sent out the message that he is not accountable. Such a person isn't trustworthy. People soon lose confidence in someone they don't trust. Your support network will pick up on these things. Even your customers will start to walk away when they stop trusting a company's products...or its intent.

Many American companies have matched this kind of honorable example, and do so today. I'm thankful for all of them, and for the success capitalism has brought our model of democracy.

The Need for Perspective

With all of this in view, it's sad that we don't show more appreciation in our lives for so many who make everything we do possible, or at least more effective. We often take full credit for performance and accomplishments without a mention or thought for support roles that provide the very basis for all we do. When we step back and look behind, we see a chain of people supporting all we do, and we have to show them we appreciate them and all they do or they might not be there next time.

To really understand this, we need to answer to (or, if you prefer, answer the question of) what our mission is, and then communicate this to our team and support network. They need to be on board with our shared vision of success. This begins by asking, "What services are or have been provided to you? What service do you provide for others?" This line of thinking engenders respect.

Now, as you look back far enough, in my opinion, you see that the ultimate form of service is represented by our relationship with our

Creator. Short of that, in any worldly sense, you'll see your mother or someone who stepped in to fill that role for you.

There isn't much that can compare to the selfless nurturing and support that a maternal figure provides. That kind of service is provided no matter the cost. She might be hungry, tired, ill, or injured, but a mother is there anyway. The best among them will put their children's needs first. That kind of love and compassion becomes the safest place in the world for us. There is evidence of this even in the end zone of an NFL playing field. It could even be during the Super Bowl, when the camera goes to a close-up shot of the touchdown-scoring player. This might very well be the highest point in that person's life, but when they know they are on camera, the most common words you'll hear will be a thank you to "Mom."

It is less apparent, but that moment exists for folks in a perilous moment too. Jesus and Mom head the list of names that get invoked in moments of imminent danger, and even death. Love and compassion are compelling, though we seldom exhibit what we should. The manliest of men still want their mothers. They know it too. When a mother and her child see each other at any age, it's typically a bond like no other.

There are deep reasons why cherished and endeared possessions most often get assigned a female name by their owners, if they are named at all. If these material things are personified, it is almost always done in female terms. I believe this goes back to the wonderful way we feel when we are being cared for and supported. Men show these selfless, supportive, and loving traits far less often than women. Culture has much to do with that, and I challenge whether our culture has been great for us overall in this respect, given that male identity in this country has largely excluded any of the seemingly feminine virtues which are obviously so good for our well-being.

Now, I realize this may be in sharp contrast to what one might expect from a career Green Beret. But, over and over in my life, I have been jolted into awareness of how love and compassion are the basis for so much that is good. Like service itself, I believe that America has fought around the world and throughout its history in support of freedom and the human condition. Americans love freedom, and we show great compassion for the human condition. You'd be hard pressed to prove to me that our motivations have been lesser ones, as I have spent 23 years as a warrior in our Army. I spent years in many countries around the world in pursuit of foreign policy interests. I've risked my life many times to pursue these ends. I have an extremely honorable feeling about my service to the United States of America. I am proud of our pursuits for freedom, security, and stability around the world, and I've seen the positive effects on populations that had not previously experienced such blessings before.

As a Special Forces Medical Sergeant, I've rendered care to people in lesser-developed places who had never seen a doctor or a dentist in their lives. I've pulled teeth for people who were miserable with dental pain. I've handed out prenatal vitamins and made small but real contributions toward reducing infant mortality rates, and even delivered babies in the absence of medical facilities. I've provided trauma management for the seriously injured and wounded. Even if we were handing out blankets or digging wells for hygienic water sources, I have always felt like we were doing great things to influence populations with love and compassion. These will surely be lifelong influences for good, efforts that create friends and allies for the future.

In the end, I attribute so much of this to a maternal nature that compels us to love, support, and to protect. It is a fight, but a justified one. If you are foolish enough to take a mother's love and compassion as weakness in any way, it can backfire on you. If you are a threat in any way to a child in a mother's care, her love and compassion will cause her to eliminate the threat. You don't want to be on the receiving end of that wrath, I assure you. The beauty in it is that her fight to safeguard a child is a justified one. She won't have to regret what she did, and she will certainly win the fight with whatever resources are available. That woman in our lives will tend to make decisions less in favor of herself and more in favor of us. I want that kind of clarity and simplicity. I want to be justified and without regret. I want my life to be meaningful and useful to others, not just selfish. I don't want to fight for the stupid reasons we often find ourselves fighting for, particularly as men. If we fight for anger, vengeance, reputation, identity, competition, or any of these lesser and selfish reasons, we are likely to regret it. It will not have been worth the fight, and it will have unlimited negative impact. But if

I fight out of love and compassion in an unselfish way, I'll never have to regret it. It will have been the right thing to do. I resolve to attach myself to feminine virtues, rather than resist them, that I may be of greater service to others, and true to the most important things in life.

I have too often witnessed ugly outcomes as a result of being too macho. Testosterone is very necessary in its natural existence, but the many ways that it is manifested outwardly in our culture aren't very productive to us, the team, or even our personal or professional support networks. There is often, in fact, a fine line between "tough" and "stupid." I will address this further in terms of team dynamics later, but, here, I'm just saying that men can be better and even fight better if they are strong enough to love in any environment.

This is not a new idea, but a fading one. Japanese Samurai warriors weren't considered complete if they didn't also practice Japanese tea ceremony or even *Ikebana*, the art of flower arrangement. Samurai were often painters in the minimalistic Japanese style. Miyamoto Musashi (1584-1645) was an expert Japanese sword master who went undefeated in his 60 duels. Musashi was the founder of the *HyōhōNitenIchi-ryū* style of swordsmanship and, in his last years, wrote a fine book on swordsmanship and philosophy, *The Book of Five Rings*. Musashi wasn't just a tough-guy swordsman; he was also an artist, a painter.

In the Western world, Spartan warriors in ancient Greece also studied music and dance. A European knight in the Middle Ages might have studied poetry or music. Even an American cavalry officer in the nineteenth century was expected to know how to dance properly, as a gentleman should, and would study poetry and the classics at West Point.

Today, our military has more often let this side of man go undeveloped. Even in popular culture, we've let how we define a soldier, or even manliness itself, become a simplistic and even boyish thing that only concentrates on stoicism and combat skills. As a soldier who spent a year and surgery after surgery in a hospital, let me tell you, if I'd developed that other side of myself, I would have had an easier time recovering, as my perspective of myself would have been more well rounded. As it was, my warrior persona had been blown away and I was left empty. I didn't know the rest of myself. I didn't even realize I wasn't well rounded. As a leader, I don't know how you can understand, appreciate, or effectively be there for and work with a support network, if you are not a well-rounded person. If you're only an alpha man or woman who charges forward without looking left, right, or behind, then, sooner or later, you're going to trip, and no one will give you cover or help you up.

It took that horrifying year in the hospital to make me aware that I have been supported more than I've supported others. Further, I feel guilty for not giving enough credit to so many who have made my success, and even survivability, possible. Being a warfighter in any capacity is a support-intensive role. It requires a much larger team than will ever be seen and recognized. Also, beyond the routine roles in any support network, dedication to the mission and to the team may dictate that one take on unanticipated duties or roles. Just ask our trusty mechanic, who found out during the Battle of Sperwan Ghar! On a great team, "that's not my job" will never be heard.

With so much being done for us, it pays to be mindful, appreciative, and mutually supportive whenever possible. That includes sharing in the success that is clearly achieved as a team. I made the mistake for years of thinking I was awesome. I was a rock, an island. Those other people don't do what I do. They don't undergo the extensive testing and training. They don't bear the risks we do. They don't face the enemy. What an arrogant ass I was. Instead of allowing such a chip to reside on my shoulder, I should have recognized the countless ways I was supported each day that made anything at all possible. I should have felt a deep obligation to be my best and do my best always for them. Instead, it took the painful experience of being wounded on the battlefield and everything that followed to put sufficient gratitude in my heart and in my attitude.

The stories of all that was done to get us more ammo and supplies on the battlefield caught up with me while I was still in a wheelchair, recovering from wounds. Great urgency was taken by so many for me. This made me re-evaluate my entire life and what service really is. I know now that to be a servant is the best identity I could ever have, and that it was never about me or my capabilities. It was about the team and the greater objectives at hand. Now I love everyone for what they do each day.

So, as leaders and team members, let's not forget that it all starts with our mother's love, and then remember those lessons and share them up and down our chains of command. It took my whole career and near death and all the pain of healing for me to finally get that. I finally see it. America isn't great because of its military. It's great because of the fabric of our culture. No one does more for our culture of service, love, and compassion than mothers. A mother makes a place a home. We only have a military because we have a culture worth defending. It's not about Fort Benning or Fort Bragg. America is about Fort Living Room. We would all be better served to remember that. Building a resilient A-Team requires a shared recognition of our values and culture. It starts in maternal love.

Too often, workplaces are only paternal. They are top-down hierarchies. A team—a family, business team, or military unit—without this selfless care gluing them together will only be a bunch of individuals out for themselves. That kind of team fails. There will be dissension and defections in a team that doesn't trust and care about one another in this way.

In the Army, there are largely paternal figures, such as the commander and the 1st sergeant. There are also roles that have a more common maternal component to them, as well. It's true that any of them can, but it's also true that they seldom do. The ones who do more frequently are the team sergeants and others who have close, caring relationships with their soldiers. More personal contact brings it on. Medics are a common example of this. It can often be tough-love, but it is always a basis of understanding. If all an A-Team had was cold, stoic paternal oversight, then it would crumble, as we are all human beings, not machines. A good A-Team understands this and, so has built a command structure where someone close enough to other members of the team knows each personality well enough to tell when something is wrong, or to know just how to communicate a problem so the team comes together behind it and doesn't fall apart into individuals because of it.

Out in the business world, if an employee or someone out in the support network doesn't feel like a boss or client has his or her back, then they won't be loyal to their boss and won't be there when a crisis comes.

In the Green Berets, command literally uses flowcharts that show visually all of the steps in a support network. It is critical for companies to do this too, as in any planning stage, it is easy to forget that you need trucking to get parts somewhere, and maybe distribution centers ready to get the product out into local markets. You need marketing to be on board too. Payroll has to be on top of it…. In the Special Forces, this means military intelligence, fuel, transportation, air support, and so much more. A team is only as strong as its weakest link. In the Green Berets, during planning sessions and practice runs, we test every link in the chain.

An August 2014 interview with the singer Pharrell Williams on *Sunday Morning* is a great example of someone who learned this the hard way. Anthony Mason interviewed Pharrell, but toward the end of the interview, Mason clearly didn't understand where Pharrell was coming from. Pharrell said, "I'm used to being the guy standing next to the guy" as he explained how he grew from a supporting role to being the lead actor. When asked how that happened, Pharrell said that after his first album, he failed to understand how he had failed, and so blamed everyone but himself. He said he later, after more failure, "realized it's not all about me. You get that, right?"

Mason said, "You are giving everyone else credit."

To this, Pharrell asks, "What am I without them?" Without help from music teachers and others in the music business, he said, "I'd have been a struggling art director; struggling because my grades were not so good."

Mason asks, "What changed for you?"

Pharrell says, "I realized along the way that there wasn't enough purpose in my music…Stevie Wonder was really singing about something." But Pharrell found he wasn't. When he realized it wasn't all about him, and so began to reach out to his team and to build relationships with them erected on mutual respect, the song "Happy" came together. This song wasn't an instant success. It didn't fit with the direction pop music was taking. But then Pharrell recorded a video for "Happy," and the song exploded overseas. It went to number one in more than 20 countries.

When asked by Mason how he feels about this, Pharrell said, "I'm thankful." And then, when Mason looked confused, Pharrell asked, "Do you get why I say that? Does it annoy you that I keep saying that?"

Mason was clearly not understanding how selflessness and giving others credit had empowered Pharrell. Mason said, "As an artist, at some point you probably tried to figure out what it is you do well."

Pharrell interrupted Mason right there to say, "I think that's when you fail...that's when you become delusional because you start to believe that...." Pharrell said talented "people spin out of control all the time—people start to believe it is really all them...just like you need air to fly a kite; it's not the kite, it's the air."

Mason was still off balance, unsure if Pharrell was being sincere or saying something just to be nice to his band and team. He was a star, after all, and, in our culture, stars are up there in the sky while the rest of us, including our support networks, are down here on earth.

This misunderstanding about a leader's role, about how a good and effective leader learns to pull strength and ideas from their team, is also common in business. In school, there are "star pupils" and "overachievers" who excel on their own merits. They graduate at the top of their classes and we forget about what their parents probably did for them and how much so many teachers and even their peers helped them. They then go into a job, and we still think of them as stars even in business; we think of them as being self-reliant. I'm not discounting self-reliance or a person's individual work ethic and ability, but when we decide, as American society has, that it's only about that person and their greatness, then we have set this poor person up for a big fall.

It wasn't always this way. The ancient Greeks thought that genius comes to us as a muse; they thought that divine things influence our greatest minds. The ancient Greeks thought some people could hear their muses clearer than others, or that some people just had better muses. The ancient Romans called these influential muses "*genius*," but not in the sense that we think of genius today. In ancient Rome, a *genius* was a guiding spirit. Some talented people were thought to have particularly powerful *geniuses* whispering deep thoughts in their ears. Later, during the European Enlightenment, came the idea of rational humanism, which dispelled this notion of muses and said it was really the person, and not some fairy with pixie dust or something, that was the genius. With that injection of rationalism, we lost a useful metaphor. When it's just us, and not some kind of divine help that's guiding us if we'll only listen, then we can easily become burdened with the idea that we can be idiots or geniuses. That's a lot of weight to put on any person. Though thinking of muses is a fanciful way of looking at where inspiration and new ideas come from, the idea had its advantages, as a person wouldn't constantly have to live up to an unrealistic label—or live down to a poor one. And he or she would stay humble as they ask their muse for help.

The idea that it is all about us is so prevalent today that, often, in business and in the military, the team captain, leader, or even a Special Forces soldier, begins to think they are the ones getting everything done, that it's all about them. Right there is the first step to neglecting a support network. Someone who starts thinking that way is going to fall, and no one will be there to catch them or help them up.

Again, this isn't to say that individual talent, work ethic, and courage don't matter. Of course they do. It's just that it's important to realize there is much more to the equation than you. You still have to be the best you can; it's just that being the best you can be includes giving credit where it is due, being humble, and appreciating all the things those in your support network are doing for you.

How to Enhance Your Support Network

What we often miss at this juncture of leadership is the human touch. We forget that maternal, not just paternal care for our troops, colleagues, or employees is what sews us together.

One of the finest people I've ever seen pull this off is a sixth-grade teacher at Trexler Middle School in Allentown, Pennsylvania. His name is John Annoni. He took a vision of what saved him while growing up in the projects and has used it to save the lives of youth who are being recruited by gangs.

John grew up without a father. His grandmother raised him. On weekends, he went to his mother's apartment in the projects. "It was a violent and abusive place," he says, "so I started going out behind the projects and hiding in this little woodlot. I'd sit there in the woods where nobody could hurt me. Pretty soon, I saw a squirrel and I started to stalk it. As time goes on, I got better at stalking and tracking game around that little woodlot. I was safe and happy there until I had to go back to the apartment—Mother Nature was saving me. Later, an uncle took me hunting, and I found a real connection to the outdoors. Guns, in this very different culture from the one I knew on the streets, helped save my life."

John started Camp Compass, an after-school program, to save inner-city kids from the bad influences of rough neighborhoods. The kids are friendly, respectful, and courteous, and they will shake your hand when you meet them and call you sir or ma'am. John has found a way to save these kids by using guns as a carrot at the end of a long stick. Learning gun safety was too politically incorrect for John's school. They told him to stop talking about guns or to leave the campus. He couldn't stop, as it was guns that were killing so many of the kids he had taught.

A friend of John's introduced him to Joe Mascari, the owner of a local carpet store. At first, when John broached the idea of having his after-school programs at Mascari's carpet store, Joe said, "Are you nuts? This is a carpet store." But John kept talking, and, pretty soon, Joe gave him some rooms to use for free.

Joe's wife had been killed by a knife-wielding murderer. "Most people would say he shouldn't be helping us because of that," says John, "but he gets it. He says if that thug had come to Camp Compass, he never would have done such an evil thing. So he helps us use guns to teach responsibility, to grow upstanding adults."

Trexler Middle School is a typical one-story, red brick building in downtown Allentown, a city of 120,000 that's an hour north of Philadelphia. Drive to it and you'll see teenagers hanging out on the streets during midday. You'll see some of those dark, sporty cars with the tinted windows and chrome hubs slowly circling city blocks. You'll see graffiti on buildings and trash bins, some from the four active gangs in the middle school.

See all this and you'll wonder, *Can this really be the place where someone uses guns to save kids' lives?*

Meeting John is meeting a man with his heart on his sleeve in everything he does. Right away, you'll know it isn't all about him, as he never talks about himself. He talks about the other teachers who help him for free, and about all the kids he sees so much potential in. John says, "Imagine Outward Bound, the Boy Scouts, Big Brothers and Big Sisters, and school all combined, and you'll start to understand how we use hunting, fishing, and shooting as rewards to create upstanding young men and women in Camp Compass Academy.

"This school used to be mostly white," John says about Trexler. "Now, after decades of 'white flight,' it's pretty diverse. So I bet you're thinking, 'Can this black guy really be helping kids by running a hunting and fishing nonprofit?'"

I smile and nod.

"A lot of students wonder at first too," he says. "New ones sometimes ask me, 'What are you?' I think they're looking for a role model they can relate to by skin color, so I reply by asking them, 'What do you think I am?' After they guess, I tell them, 'I'm half black and half white, but I look Spanish and I eat Chinese food.' They laugh. I let them all know I'm just like them."

No doubt about it, he's a straight shooter.

He rolls on, "If someone told me I'd be doing what you're about to see 20 years ago, I'd have said they were crazy. But the few chances I got to hunt as a kid helped me, so I figured it could help others too. So, 17 years ago, I started down this path by just taking a few kids out. We now have 60 students enrolled. We have a waiting list of 300. I mentor a lot online too. I just don't have the resources to take more students on right now. We're a nonprofit. Every dime we raise helps these kids. But that's all I'm going to tell you. It'll be clearer if I show you."

At Joe Mascari's Carpets & Rugs, we go in the back door, past displays of tiles and rugs, and enter a classroom with four long tables and lots of chairs. Half the tables are already filled with students. They're all dutifully working on a written assignment. They have on hunter orange Camp Compass Academy t-shirts. As more students arrive, they know just what to do: Get the assignment and go to work. Each must begin by picking up a wooden gunstock with a scope taped to it. They have to look out a window through the riflescope and read a quote taped to the bus. Today the quote reads, "It doesn't matter how slow you go as long as you don't stop. —Confucius." They have to write down and memorize the quote.

In an adjacent room is Russ Reigel, a retired social studies teacher, inputting students' school grades into a computer. The students are required to share their report cards with the Camp Compass Academy staff. Reigel, Annoni, and a few other volunteer teachers then look for weak areas in each student's education. If students don't get their grades up, they won't get to go hunting or fishing, so most do.

Most students have to be in the program for two years before they can go on a hunt. In the meantime, they learn about firearm safety and the wildlife they'll hunt. They also study the science behind hunting and try things like fly-tying, taxidermy, and turkey calling.

At one table are a few students, and I ask if any of them had ever hunted before they got into Camp Compass Academy. They all say they hadn't even thought about hunting, but say they all now want to go.

Jay, a freshman in high school, says she had no idea what an elk or antelope was before getting into the program. She's been involved since she was in sixth grade.

"Now I know gun safety and how to shoot," she says. "I have respect for wildlife because of hunting. Also, I've learned a lot about science. When I got my first deer, I couldn't believe how much its parts really looked like the scientific drawings."

"Did you eat your deer?" I ask.

"Yeah," she says, "venison is tasty."

Across from her is Anthony. He is in the eighth grade. He's the one who shook my hand back in the school. He has taken deer and a bear.

When I ask if anyone at home hunts, they all say "no," and Jay adds, "My mom is afraid of guns. At first, she thought this was really weird, but now she thinks it's cool."

I stand up as Jay says to a few girls beside her that she wants to kill a bear and put the bear rug in her bedroom, but that she could never wear fur. One of the other girls thinks that's a contradiction and begins to tease her about it. "How can you have a bear rug but be against wearing fur?" They're all laughing and figuring that out.

A young man—a graduate—has come in, and I want to talk to him. His name is Tracy. He's 19 years old. He shakes my hand.

"I come here to get away from the streets, you know," he says. "I like huntin' because when you're out there, you're safe. No one is giving you trouble or somethin'."

Annoni steps over and puts his hand on Tracy's shoulder. "You doin' all right with that job?" he asks quietly.

"Yeah, good for now," says Tracy.

John is called away, and I ask Tracy what the program did for him.

"Kind of saved my life, I guess," he says with this quiet seriousness that makes me worry about him a little, but I can see that if things go wrong, he'll reach out to John and find his way back to the positive path he began at Camp Compass Academy. That has happened often over the years for a lot of kids.

John Annoni says he doesn't take the top students—"They're already getting enough love," he says—and he can't take those who won't take his help. He takes kids who need Camp Compass Academy, those whom he thinks he can help.

What John has is heart. It's his passion that has brought his team together. He knows it's not all about him, even though all of his team members jump when he does. John couldn't run it by himself. He couldn't do all the data entry and a thousand other tasks that are out of his expertise or that don't suit his nature. Sure, he is running an after-school program, not a business or a military unit. But I'd say that what he is doing is actually harder, as there is no template to follow. He can't recruit or hire a team that already knows how to play the game. He has to articulate and live the vision and then look to others to grasp this and help and even teach him how to do it better.

John Annoni is a man who understands both the paternal and maternal parts of what a leader should be. He is not a man who would neglect his support network.

PART TWO
READYING THE TEAM, WEAPONS, AND EQUIPMENT

"In place of maps, whiteboards began to appear in our headquarters. Soon they were everywhere. Standing around them, markers in hand, we thought out loud, diagramming what we knew, what we suspected, and what we did not know. We covered the bright white surfaces with multicolored words and drawings, erased, and then covered again. We did not draw static geographic features; we drew mutable relationships—the connections between things rather than the things themselves."

—GENERAL STANLEY McCHRYSTAL

5

HOW TO BUILD YOUR A-TEAM

Diversity Is Only Strong When the Differently Shaped Parts Fit Together as a Puzzle

"We are what we pretend to be, so we must be careful
about what we pretend to be."

—KURT VONNEGUT

Maybe you are into sports and remember how the Boston Red Sox came back in the 2004 American League Championship series to become a team no one could beat after being down three games to none in the seven-game series against the Yankees. Or maybe you think of the Chicago Bulls in the 1995–1996 season with Michael Jordan at his best with Dennis Rodman, Randy Brown, and more. What you are thinking of are likely the stars and the coaches, sure, but beyond even them is a team that suddenly plays like a team, as if each player fits seamlessly with his or her teammates. How do you recruit and develop a team of individuals, maybe of exceptional individuals, into one tight unit moving down the battlefield, field of play, or business sector expertly?

Common perception is that the best or winning team is simply a collection of the best players. In the Green Berets, I have learned that's not true. It is common to see talents not fully utilized on a team. It's also common in the workplace to see the best subject-matter expert in a leadership role even though they don't have the skills to lead. Leadership and operation knowledge are entirely different things, with challenges inherent to both roles that have nothing to do with actual tasks at hand.

Anyone who's ever had a boss who isn't good with people knows what I mean already. Someone might be a great welder or a great accountant, but they aren't necessarily the right person to manage operations or lead the team. They might actually be the best in the world at what they do—yet still shouldn't be a team leader.

In the Green Berets, I was part of a method for building teams that had been honed to a razor's edge. When I think about this I recall some Green Beret A-Teams I served on. Actually, I see the Green Beret A-Teams I served differently in hindsight. At the time, I was so deep into the details, into the Green Beret method I'll tell you about here, that I was also missing the big picture that can help you in your private life and career.

Of course, we did some things together I can't tell you about, but it's the method that we're after, not the particulars of any mission.

First, let me warn you, how the Green Berets build a team—and how start-up businesses flourish and how small-budget sports teams can surprise everyone by winning championships—can seem counterintuitive, even as if they are exceptions. But in my experience, these are not anomalies. They are teams that broke the norms to get something right. The keys to putting together a team to accomplish a goal begins first with the fundamentals we already talked about—having a code, a defined mission...—but at this stage picking or recruiting an A-Team has more to do with breaking free from political correctness, from bias, and even from things you've been taught so you can see what makes every part (every team member) valuable or problematic. This doesn't just have to do with individual prowess, but also with how these parts fit together.

Now, the methodology behind picking the right team has been dramatized in movies like the 1967 film *The Dirty Dozen*, starring Lee Marvin, and even by the 1980s television show *The A-Team*, which was supposed to be about a rogue team of Green Berets working to do good as they tried to clear their names. Perhaps the best sequence of scenes showing the recruitment of a diverse and incredible team was done by writer and director Akira Kurosawa in his 1954 epic *The Seven Samurai*. Those examples, however, show but don't tell. Here's the real, intricate process for recruiting a team that doesn't just look good on paper, but that can achieve the objective.

If you are worried that the Green Beret method I'm explaining here might not be relevant to the team you are building to succeed in business or life, don't be. There are more parallels than exceptions. And many business leaders have nodded along as I've related my insights to them before telling me I'd got to the heart of what they have often found and try to say.

Chris Zarpas, who, as vice president of production and acquisitions at the Walt Disney Company, developed and supervised numerous motion pictures including "Beaches" starring Bette Midler, and later, as co-president of Island Pictures in Los Angeles, produced "Toy Soldiers" for Tri Star, "Strictly Business" for Warner Bros. and "Sandlot" for Fox, had this to say:

> "We all take flying for granted. But when you think about it, a commercial jet liner is 100 tons of sheet metal and wire. That it can somehow fly through the air, transporting 150 people from NY to Paris seems impossible. It's awe inspiring.
>
> "A movie is very similar. It starts as only 120 8.5×11 pieces of paper. And then 250 people (the crew) who have never met one another, assemble together at some distant location and 6–9 months later, a great movie results. The team is hand-picked and led by the producer according to a variety of variables, such as the relative stature and experience of the director, budget size, genre, etc. There are many military parallels."

The Green Beret Method

I have been a part of many efforts to select the perfect A-Team for certain missions. By the time a team is selected to perform highly specified tasks a long, persistent, and redundant assessment and selection process has been utilized in order to build the right teams to choose from.

In the Special Forces (SF) it is understood that assessment never ends. We say this because any SF career begins with the assessment and selection course "Define Assessment." All candidates are assessed, but few are selected. The assessment and selection process goes on in perpetuity because having a minimum qualification to become a Green Beret to start with doesn't mean that any team member is best suited for any given mission. It also does not count for so many changes that people go through. A person's current disposition matters too.

Our Special Operations units are the best in the world partly because of constant reassessment. It is not enough to say that you accomplished something in the past and so *deserve* to be on the next team. What you did before doesn't necessarily qualify you for what's to come. A person's posture, attitude, and motivation change. This goes for Green Berets too. Among the best, there are still better and lesser picks. It is not disrespectful to anyone to make the most appropriate selection we can. By all means we need to use tact, but we still need to sort people out for success.

Our objectives in life and business vary. Whether we are choosing someone to be a business partner or an employee, questions need to be answered to satisfy the objectives and requirements at hand. We hope the people in the positions last as well, as we are investing in them.

So we start with honest questions. Who would you select as a work partner? Would that be the same person you'd pick to care for your ailing mother? Who would you select to help you with a marketing plan? Would they also be best to provide physical security for you or your property? The variables are infinite. What makes it even harder is that our choices among available people are few in most cases. That is an advantage the military has; they have a bunch of people who are qualified for the tasks at hand. The people are trained and somewhat vetted already. This is something I miss about life in the military, but what I learned there helps me greatly now that I'm a civilian.

In the Special Forces, our membership was based on working and training hard. We did this in order to remain in contention for the biggest missions that might come down. *Pick me! Pick me!* Those words weren't spoken as such, but that was the overall feeling and motivation. Each A-Team works very hard on fundamental skills and physical fitness in order to gain maximum consideration when the nation needs something dangerous done. So the teams are in competition with one another. Some businesses have set up new product-development departments like this—with competing teams all trying to get chosen.

On a Green Beret A-Team no matter how jovial things get there is always a very serious and sober undertone that remains present to usher in the reality that what we do next may cost us our lives. They know the stakes and all say goodbye to fallen brothers. This makes it easier to maintain clarity and candor in the assessment and selection process. We know how to tell you no, even if we love you. Fortunately, for all of us, life-and-death standards don't have to be met each day. Still, most of us want to make the best decisions and choices for success and quality of life.

Memories of individual and team selections weigh heavily on the decisions I make today. Individual selections for specific roles are less common in the Special Forces, in terms of missions. They operate fundamentally on a team-based structure; however, there will always be an SF guy or two in places and positions the public won't be aware of. When one of those roles is necessary to fill, it needs serious consideration for who is best to do it. I remember hearing about legendary actions taken by a fellow Green Beret during the onset of the Albanian Civil War in 1997 who was serving in a lesser-known capacity without an A-Team.

When a series of large Ponzi schemes ran their course in Albania, and so many lost their money, the government had no real answer for it. The result was an uprising of great magnitude and civil war. When over a million weapons were taken from federal arsenals, the violence that followed resulted in approximately 2,000 deaths. At the time, there was a Green Beret named Blake there who made all the difference for a large number of Americans and their families. His selection had been important, and it made perfect sense to me after closely observing him every chance I got. I wanted to be like him. I wanted to save the day too.

Blake was a guy I'd been made aware of before I met him, and I saw him awarded for amazing things he'd done before we ever spoke. Until this time, my military career had not taken me to what I considered to be a culmination of my training and education. I had certainly been around and seen some things, but not to the degree I'd fantasized. That's not a death wish, but every Green Beret really wants to earn his pay. Blake had been around the block, and I paid close attention to everything he said and did. I doubt my young punk ego would have allowed him to know he was a mentor to me. I was so busy trying to measure up all the time that I just didn't reach out enough to make it apparent what certain people meant to me. Anyway, Blake had been the guy who helped save American citizens from the violence through an amazing evacuation of our embassy there.

The evacuation is known as "Operation Silver Wake" and took place in March 1997. The operation was primarily performed by U.S. Marines from the 26th Marine Expeditionary Unit conducting operations from the USS *Nassau* Amphibious Readiness Group. U.S. Marines from 1st Battalion, 8th Marines secured the U.S. housing compound and held the U.S. Embassy. Over 900 personnel were evacuated during the course of the operation. Blake was a quiet professional behind the scenes pulling the parts of the evacuation together.

Watching Blake day by day, doing his job in the company area, captured my imagination. Blake never spoke of the great things he'd done. If someone mentioned them, he would always be too busy with things at hand or would make himself busy, rather than entertain a conversation about himself. I saw him routinely immersing himself in the business of the day, preparing for training and combat, completing administrative tasks, doing physical training, and training and teaching younger guys like me. He never once sought credit or attention. He kept his head. I still don't think I would have been able to prevent seeking attention for myself if I were him. I studied him and longed for that kind of focus and maturity. He didn't know it, but he was teaching me. This guy was not only professional and mature, but he was kind and courteous to everyone, easy to get along with, and quick to volunteer for anything that needed doing. Though I wasn't anywhere near the selection process for his position in Albania, it was easy to see what the considerations had been picking him. I bet it made all the difference. He needed to be the ultimate warrior to handle that situation, but the ultimate gentleman and diplomat to maintain great daily rapport to lead civilians out of peril in a way that I am certain made them want to follow Blake.

Blake taught me that, as we fit human pieces into our functional puzzles, it is wise not to plan for best-case scenarios. To the contrary, wisdom dictates that we plan for worst-case scenarios. That certainly adds a lot of reality to our selection processes.

Building, assessing, and selecting the right team isn't as brief a process as selecting an individual. The examples of this are countless, but some really stand out for me. Most of us can't just pick from teams that are already functioning together. Our efforts more often have us selecting folks as we go to build teams in our respective applications. Either way, building your A-Team depends on assessing individuals and selecting them to meet a range of requirements. This is where diversity matters most to me. People of all kinds are a true blessing, as they bring such a wide range of capabilities and competencies. Our unique cultures, ethnicities, and more bring specific familiarities with them, not always shared by others. Many of these traits, experiences, and abilities aren't readily apparent in somewhat sterile everyday environments, but when things get either very comfortable or very uncomfortable, we find out what we didn't realize about others and ourselves. In my experience, this produces much more joy than horror, and it is very important to understand the potential assets that diversity gives us.

On one mission, a requirement was to penetrate the security of a storage facility and extract a sample from a collection of what was estimated to be 55-gallon drums. None of us had the industrial experience to know what different types of opening devices might be necessary to gain access to the contents. We needed to do so without breaching a barrel with munitions or brute force. Anyway, what was in the barrels could have killed us all, so we needed to rely on cool heads and cool hands for the mission. We also needed a certain industrial wherewithal or competency for this specific task. We either needed someone who knew how to do this to go with us or someone to teach us. We found someone to teach us how to open the barrels properly. We mastered the skill and took that knowledge with us.

On another mission, a clear contingency for getting outta there became hotwiring a certain type of car. Those aren't everyday competencies and they take you outside of your normal selection process. We literally had to find people who really knew how to quickly and efficiently hotwire a car.

Often, there was a key person that would be the focus of our actions or activities. In these cases, it always helped to find commonality between the team and that key person. This usually came down to one or two people who had that common thread and could be counted on to do well with communication and interpersonal skills. If the only discernible commonality happened to be a passion for beekeeping, then we needed someone to be able to talk shop with personal interest in beekeeping. That's a true story, by the way. These specifics in no way take away from the need for shared values, standards, and objectives among the members of a team. They only add to the complexity of team building and leadership.

The "I" in Team

A lot of attention has been given to the notion of knowing yourself in order to be a good leader or teammate. This is absolutely the starting point for each person, for each leader, and for each team. I don't like how a lot of folks go about it, though. Honestly, hearing people describe themselves is often painful. I hope I don't sound like the biggest jerk in the world when I say that, but if you've ever heard the elaborate "I'm a winner" way people pump themselves full of sunshine, you know what I mean. Too often, when I hear people describe themselves, it sounds like they've been to a Stuart Smalley self-help workshop. Certainly, there are good traits in all of us. It pays to recognize those things. But should that be the way we describe ourselves? While we do love ourselves, in general, love of self should never be what one leads with in a self-description. If a person is fixated on his or her own wonderful attributes in their approach to a team, then it is seldom an indicator of good things to come. For all we think we know about ourselves, the impressions that others have are often very different than our own. In addition, it is incomplete to go through life focused only on what we know, as that blinds us and leaves us open to making arrogant mistakes. To be less selfish, it is better to show concern for what we don't know, and to remain open to the knowledge of others.

It is true that our nature tends to be selfish. As humans, our most basic instincts are related to the drive to survive and reproduce. Unfortunately, that selfish nature is automatic. Lesser qualities in people are most often tied to primal nature that disregards more developed and civilized behavior. These characteristics and behaviors are most often tied to a focus on the self and a disregard for others. On the extreme side of this reality, criminality results. A day in criminal court is revealing, in terms of what people do to others while focused entirely on themselves and what they want in any given moment. To be selfish is easy. What takes real team development for most of us is being unselfish.

At the other end of the spectrum is a great leader. A great leader is last in line to eat. They make sure everyone is fed and that the needs of the team are met before they allow themselves to partake. Typically, a good way to look at it is that a great leader will be in front to face challenge and hardship, but to the rear in accepting comfort, pleasure, or privilege. While it's true that the position will necessarily put the leader in environments and situations not shared by the team, it is imperative that favorable conditions afforded remain in the context and purpose of promoting team success and wellbeing. Avoiding our basic selfish nature is inherent to becoming a valuable team player and imperative to becoming a good leader.

The effort for growth and self-improvement is necessary for people of conscience. It is also necessary to be a good team member. One should get tired of making the same mistakes repeatedly, and especially having to explain it and remain accountable to others for those mistakes. In my life and experience, the best way to make consistent gains in that pursuit is to confirm the set of values we believe in. When we stay grounded in those core values, they will help steer us through everything in life. In terms of building a team, the values of each individual will make enormous differences in the ability of the group to be unified in meaningful ways. This creates a real priority in selection criteria.

Building your A-Team needs to be driven by an ethic that can be supported by each member, and they all have to be committed to a common goal. To be aligned in a team dynamic in no way limits diversity, however. To the contrary, I've seen amazing team dynamics and capabilities extended and improved by diversity itself. I am a white man, and it has nothing to do with white guilt, but I happen to love diversity. But putting diversity to work for me is not the same as the world of political correctness sees it.

will be exposed, and it will be revealed that you aren't as good as you said. Worse, you will fail the team. You will fail the team that counted on you to do the thing they just knew you were great at because you said you were. They may have pushed aside others who are competent to let you lead the way because of the false confidence you instilled in others for your abilities.

The example that always comes to mind for me is the guy who acts tough all the time. He acts smart. He's never surprised by anything said to him, or at least he works hard to never look surprised. He knows it all and he's done it all. One of these jerks was someone I looked up to in the Army. I was inspired by the confidence he showed all the time. It made me believe that he'd done it all. It made me feel like I should watch and learn from him, because I didn't want to be nervous or afraid anymore. He could show me how to be better and stronger, without the need for all this cumbersome anxiety I felt about performing in combat. Looking back now, I see things differently. Anyone who doesn't own up to their own humanity worries me now. I feel like it will be an ugly "crash-and-burn" experience when they fail.

I've learned that a guy like that is setting himself up for a very big problem. In this particular case—I'll call him Sergeant Z—I'm quite sure this person actually believed he was that tough. He presented the tough-guy image for so long, or "faking the funk," that I think he even fooled himself.

Then came the enemy fire in battle. The same gunfire he claimed to have endured and overcome through bravery and superior tactics many times over. In the first volley of gunfire, Sergeant Z magically disappeared. As I returned fire at the enemy, feeling fear, anger, and an entire cocktail of human emotions, I noticed Sergeant Z wasn't shooting. In my mind's eye, he was being brave and stealthy to gain some superiority over our enemy. He was being his badass self to win the fight on our behalf. Somehow, I felt that whatever he was doing would ultimately save me and take down the enemy. It did not occur to me that Z would be back inside the vehicle on the floor in a fetal position, curled up around an ammo can, and crying.

When I found him there, I was in shock more from that, than I had been from the live combat action at hand. This was the man I'd been modeling myself after. The one I could learn from. It wasn't the cool swagger I was after, but presence that comes from competency. That's what I thought he had. The result of his false confidence created a major failure that put lives in danger. He not only became inert in a firefight, but he increased the odds of fatalities overall. He had denied his own fear. He didn't deal with the realities of being human. Instead, in the moment of truth, his fear dealt with him. By the time he actually felt the fear, he didn't know how to manage it and it consumed him.

I'd rather pick the 98-pound weakling who is crying *before* the fight begins. He has a tear running down his cheek and a quivering boo boo lip, as he shamefully says to me, "Sarge, I don't think I can do this." That kid is dealing with real human feelings, and we all have them. By the time the enemy starts shooting, that young man is embarrassed about crying and has been feeling ashamed. But now he's pissed. That 98-pound weakling may become the next Audie Murphy, because now he's fighting like 10 men, while the big tough guy over there is just now dealing with real fear, and it's suppressing his abilities in a critical moment. Being honest with ourselves and one another makes a difference. Especially when it counts.

In the Army's Airborne School at Fort Benning in 1992, I learned a couple of valuable lessons. One was the value of rehearsals. You see, when your life depends on it in a moment that can overpower your senses and sensibilities, rehearsals can be the only thing you have going for you. The repetitive exercises we do can stick in our minds, becoming handrails and a survival mechanism. Jumping out of an airplane isn't the smartest thing to do, let's face it. It can get you killed. So when the door opens in flight, and you hear the noise and feel the wind, very primal fears are provoked. That's the first time I can recall rehearsals having such significance. Not like a music recital or graduation ceremony.

In some circumstances, we can get overcome and reach a threshold. It is a mistake, however, to believe that because you didn't respond well to certain stimuli once, you will always have that limitation. We can all be conditioned. That moment when fear or confusion overwhelms us is unforgettable, and we are all hopeful that no one bears witness to our time of weakness and limitation. It is nonetheless human. This brings me to another lesson I learned. It was when the door opened on the side of the plane I was riding in while in flight.

I cringed with the realization that a door big enough to walk through had been deliberately opened while our airplane was flying. I knew that this was the name of the game. I knew all the steps. I knew why that foolish person was leaning out the open door—to spot the drop zone. I "knew" everything I was supposed to know. That did not exempt me from feeling hesitation about what I was doing. It didn't give me a way to not feel fear. I would never have admitted it, though. I did quite a bit to conceal my fear and hesitation. I wanted to exude confidence and courage among my peers. When the guy beside me started losing his composure, I am embarrassed that I acted in insulting ways. I turned away like I was ashamed of him. I treated him like it was silly to be afraid, while I did my best to hide my own fear. He began crying as he was gripped with thoughts of his own mortality and failure. The biggest dude on the plane with us was a guy named Brandon. We were all early in the long process of trying to put ourselves in contention for the Green Beret at this time, and everyone had their guard up. Everyone had something to prove. But Brandon defied all the "man rules" and even safety considerations to come to the side of this guy I was treating like a leper. Brandon sat beside him and held his hand. *Held his hand.* I could hear his words to the fearful guy. It was nothing but encouragement about how we had all done what it takes to be ready for this together, and that he was a little scared too.

I heard him say, "You're ready for this, man!"

Brandon got up and faced him, putting helmet to helmet. With one last squeeze of the hand and a pat on the shoulder, the gentle giant returned to his own seat on the webbing of the plane. The guy next to me was toughening up now. No one else said a word to him. He found the resolve from that wonderful gesture to gather his nerve again and drive on. That guy clearly relied on rehearsals to overcome big stuff that day, because he fell right in line and made no mistakes as he exited the aircraft in a series of specific steps to fall toward earth, waiting for a paper-thin layer of silk to save him.

If he hadn't jumped, he would have been considered a jump refusal, resulting in his ejection from the program. Because of a team player like Brandon, nothing stopped this soldier's great combat arms career. Because of Brandon, I learned how to be more of a real man and a better team player. For all of us on that plane that day: thank you, Brandon.

Keeping a focus on what we are already good at, doesn't allow for much improvement. Real improvement comes when we acknowledge what we aren't good at, and go to work on it. On any team, it pays to be intimate enough with one another to confess our limitations and weaknesses. Just like in the days of soldiering with swords and shields, we all have a weak side. We need our buddy to cover that weakness, as we cover theirs. Allow iron to sharpen iron, by exposing the things that need work and improving them together. This will raise the bar in overall performance.

My golf instructor taught me a lot about raising that bar. Yes, I said golf instructor. To most who have known me, golf would never be something I considered doing. They were right until recently. Echoes of Chief Stube's (my father's) voice and current interests had me taking a look at golf for the first time. Just what was all the fuss about, chasing little white balls around with clubs? I would finally see what compels folks to waste all that beautiful property. Between the victorious fist pumping and club-launching fits of rage I'd seen from golfers on TV, I knew that, at least, golf could involve a bit of passion. Some had told me I really should play, that it's great for a person. Wiser old golfers told me it's the pursuit of fools; that it would create hate and discontent never to be overcome. Their humor and satire for the game intrigued me. My dad simply said that if I were smart, I'd play golf.

So there I was, at a golf course, and here I am including details of it in my description of how to build an A-Team. Bear with me. For all of my new curiosity, it came down to one person. One man would show me the game and how to play it. It would be the local golf pro, Ron Dinges. I was warned he could be a little gruff, but I felt like I'd probably dealt with worse. For the first time in a long time, I was starting something I knew absolutely nothing about. I was a babe in the woods. It has never been my style to approach anything halfway. I drove to the course with a studious mind and a humble attitude, hoping to come out with something as good in my life as golf seemed to be for others.

Ron greeted me in a way that made me curious how others thought he was gruff. That warm and friendly demeanor continued, but during the third lesson I got a look at the tougher side of Ron Dinges. That tougher side has a lot to do with standards. It turns out that Ron knows a great deal about standards, because not only is he a golf pro, he happens to have retired from a career in the U.S. Air Force. I liked it. He was using terms I could relate to, with an adherence to high standards. Still, after my full career in the Special Forces, what would this golf instructor have that could help me understand about raising the bar in overall performance? Everything. This is why it's true that we should never stop learning. There's so much to gain from, and golf lessons with this man triggered a new awareness in me.

In the third lesson, I think I saw Ron gritting his teeth a bit with a little frustration. At one point in the lesson, I'm not really sure what he said, but this is what I heard. "Just put the club down. Just put it down and stand there for a minute. Stube, stop trying to kill it. Stop trying to worry so much about your best shot!"

This is where I know exactly what he said, because it put a new light on everything I've done, and it changed how I'll approach the rest of my life. Ron calmly said, "It's not how good your best shot is that counts. It is more about just how bad your bad ones are."

He then said, "You have to slow down and focus on fundamentals for each shot, so that when you make inevitable mistakes, they won't cause absolute failure. Then you wind up with an average of much better shots. The one great shot you make will not make you a better golfer. Everyone gets lucky once in a while. But by raising the lower end of your game, you are incorporating standards and fundamentals that are more consistent and predictable. Only then do you have a real chance at being good at this."

I guess most of us would love to be hotshots in some way. I'm no exception. Focusing on basics is better, though, because it builds something that lasts and continues to support the objective.

Getting the Kinks Out of a Team

Thinking outside the box seems to be a popular concept right now. There seems to be a million ninjas out there in any given career field. Just look at blogs. The experts are everywhere. But I say that we are better as individuals and as teammates if we focus less on getting outside the box, and get back into rehearsing fundamentals in any discipline. I believe that Murphy lives outside the box. We are more prone to making big errors while trying to be too advanced in what we do. We all know about Murphy's Law, but I've seen where he stays much of the time. He's standing right outside the box with a big stick, just waiting for you to act like you're better than you are. In the military we say, "Slow is smooth, and smooth is fast." This means that by rehearsing at a slow speed, one becomes much more familiar with proper form and movement. With those mechanics so well-rehearsed and reinforced, the smoothness of your slow movements allow them to naturally speed up, maintaining proper fundamentals with amazing speed all from focusing on going slow.

It's just best if we all humble ourselves and stick to basics. Great things will still come, but they will be well-founded and more sustainable that way. Letting iron sharpen iron on your team will necessitate the intimacy that will lead to trust and overall competency.

Selection may be the most critical element of building a team. Without it, we don't have a team at all. We all go through some kind of selection in life. As children, we all pick teams in sports for physical education in school. Beyond that, there are tryouts for everything. Band, sports teams, chorus, and even the school play has a selection process to it. Many of these activities give us the basics for how to put a team together. Such common activities based on fun or extra-curricular programs are of less consequence in life than careers or other aspirations, whether short or long-term.

The importance of team dynamics is first witnessed for many young people in these early social practices. It is normal to see individuals with less motivation in these activities as children. In fact, it is normal occasionally to see a child who doesn't want to be there at all. Usually it is because a parent wants them to participate and it was not their choice to be there. Sometimes it has to do with a simple change of heart or a bad day. This is okay when there's nothing significant hanging on the success or failure of the team.

It can actually be fun to observe the attitudes and conduct of youthful players and participants. This changes as we get older and the stakes get higher. It is no longer funny to witness apathy when motivation should be there. When folks are investing in a desired outcome, they stand to lose something due to a lack of performance on the part of even a single member of a team. This is where selection becomes more important. This is where the nature and origin of one's motivation plays a key role. So much more about a person's culture, upbringing, attitude, and other factors come into view while trying to form and maintain a team that will push hard consistently to succeed, cooperate, and communicate, and win against adversity.

Building a team is a journey that requires some of the most complex navigation. Navigation of human terrain is what I mean. Most jobs are not so hard to do. They are mostly straightforward. What often makes a job challenging is often more to do with personality issues. The characters at play make our work easy or hard, in general. Poor leadership, blame games, laziness, jealousy, disrespect, and other human obstacles are what typically present the most challenges in what we do. As this only applies where humans are involved, it can make hermits of us. We can become a bit antisocial. We don't have to be down about it, though. It is better to accept these challenges and joyfully steer into them, excited about positive effects we might be able to have. Each of us has the power to improve the dynamic of our whole team. Most often, however, it requires a great deal of patience, understanding, and compassion.

Of the challenges I mentioned, poor leadership is the most common issue, and presents the widest variety of problems. For this reason, leadership cannot be treated as something independent of team dynamics. It often stands as the origin of or the driving force for team dynamics, so its importance therein can't be overstated. It is also important to acknowledge that most leadership competencies are developed within the culture and dynamics of team involvement. To me, all this suggests that some focus and effort need to go into the selection of team members and leaders. Prepare to navigate the human terrain.

Ask What Motivates Possible Team Members

What motivates a person? Does it come from inside their own mind and heart, or is it something they derive from external influence? What does it take for that person to maintain focus on that motivation? Whether it comes from something in a person's childhood that compels them forward, or something they want out of each day, or things they are driving for in the future and hoping to achieve, it helps to be able to identify what it is. It definitely helps them to know, but in the construction of a resilient team, you will need to be able to determine that for yourself, in general, for each person. Some people need a slight push, some need strong reminders, while others don't need anything more than the objective at hand. It pays to know the difference. Particularly in high performance environments, wide diversity coupled with strong will creates its own leadership challenges. It's often described as "herding kitty cats." Even among type "A" personalities and top performers, they may have less in common than you'd think and be driven very uniquely, each one.

In the Special Forces, there is a fairly common thread among the operators. That thread is largely based on high performance orientation that has been professionally established and, typically, validated often. We know the motivation is there, right? But what motivates each person can be shockingly different. What exists outside of that common thread is often better not discussed sometimes, as it challenges our core values or patriotic image of what warfighters are, and what drives them. Truth is, every walk of life harbors individuals who shock us once they're exposed or revealed. Let's face it, some of our most notorious characters in history have come from quiet neighborhoods and even church communities. Just natural law in the cross section of any population will dictate almost certain anomalies. The Special Forces was no exception to this rule, and I was mortified at times as my idealism and naivety was challenged by the nature of certain individuals. This didn't mean bad things were being done. It means that while the same objectives are being sought and achieved, and the same high performance and standards are being maintained, motivations could vary wildly. Knowing that such variance exists among seemingly similar people is important to know in team development and leadership. The good news is that you don't have to share everything in life with everyone.

Once again, navigating this sort of human terrain will be the biggest part of building your A-Team. When we make choices regarding friends, co-workers, teammates, and any other relationship, professional or personal, we must look at the dispositions, attitudes, and motivations of others. This includes not only a person's talents, but the nature and tendencies in their application of those talents. To be good at the selection process, we must limit our nature to be too critical of others. Maintaining enough objectivity to disregard perceived differences is key to harnessing our absolute commonalities. More often, the commonalities far outweigh the perceived differences. Yet, it is human nature to assess negatively, when we see and hear things that don't seem to match our own cultural perspective or personal leanings. As challenging as it can be to be fair or favorable to people with differences, the other side is no easier. For many people, using candor is difficult. Denying, rejecting, or excluding someone feels hard. Especially someone you know. The hard truth is that choosing who does not make the team is at least as important as choosing who does.

Choosing who makes our A-Team feels easy at first. There's a warm feeling we get from the whole notion of our own team, and it can soften us to make less careful decisions. There really isn't one step to character assessment. We sometimes must pay a high price through the trial and error in our lives. Many of us have "found out who your friends are." Those revelations can be damaging and hurtful.

Everyone concerned may pay a price for a choice. A poor selection for a team member may even cause a mission to fail. Meanwhile, you can also be criticized if you don't choose a certain person; some will say this means you're crude, or you think you're better than others. Sound familiar? There's not really a good way to exclude others. You just have to have the guts to do it when necessary.

As my father, who I always called "The Chief," always told me: "Show me your friends, and I'll show you your future." I couldn't see it then, but I do now. He meant it personally, but it applies professionally as well. When lives were on the line, it's funny how my ability to sort out bad apples became easy. Otherwise, we sort of act like it's not so important, rather than face the prospect of "non-selecting" someone. We should all remember that when we start blaming others, instead of taking responsibility ourselves. Particularly in leadership, it is paramount to understand that we can delegate authority all day long, but we can never delegate responsibility. This points right back to surrounding ourselves with the right people in the first place or try to do it all ourselves because we can't trust people enough to delegate effectively. So it seems we can either be a jerk on the front end, or be responsible for failure, or at least hardship, on some level, in the end.

Choosing people we know is not always best. Though a known entity may feel better and more comfortable, we may overlook shortcomings and incompatibilities in them that we would never accept from an outsider. It may be hard to find the words to say to reject them, but it is necessary if you want to build a real A-Team around you. Never forget the objective at hand, and never forget your responsibility and obligation to that end.

I knew a guy named Rob. We went to Special Forces Assessment and Selection together in 1992. He quit, and was immediately reassigned based on the needs of the Army at the time. I'll never forget how he acted before the tough training started. His mouth apparently carried him through everything. His loud Boston accent pierced any environment, and gave the impression of confidence with it. He spoke in very manly ways and presented himself as an alpha male posture, among others. We had become buddies, though, and were spending time together, and I grew to like him. I even watched him and listened to him to try to gain confidence that I lacked. He had it, so I followed him. Then he quit the thing we were there to do. He just quit. When the going got tough, there was just a paper tiger there.

I saw him again in 2005. He showed up at Ft. Bragg as a Major with assignment to Civil Affairs. Apparently, he had gone through a commissioning program to become an officer. It was exciting to see him again. Memories flooded in from times that were exciting, nervous, painful, and trying, but also victorious for me. Our shared times from a long time ago seemed to foster an affinity between us. We had something in common. My description of that shared time includes the word "victorious." I think it's fair to say that Rob's description of that time would not.

The words you hear most often going into Special Forces testing and training are, "don't quit." Everything about the program is voluntary, so from the perspective of any pool of candidates, quitting is actually a realistic option. Many consider it from the start, and most of those don't make it very far. Those who do quit are never treated poorly by the cadre. To the contrary, they are often afforded absolute relative privilege. The understanding that Special Forces is not for everyone is the most obvious reason for that. Attrition is the constant in this environment, and as a community, an appreciation is always present for the willingness of these candidates to come suffer in the attempt to become an operator. Beyond the obvious, it is often good to treat the quitters well because it can tip the scales with many on the verge of giving up. The sight of comfort, rest, good and plentiful food, and recreation is quite tempting during times the absence of these things is compounded by fatigue, discomfort, no personal time, and sleep deprivation. When a guy sees these things during tough times, it causes a re-assessment of his decision to volunteer for such tough stuff. The same can be said for any person in life whose commitment is tested. Something worth serving should be worth serving above self. Serving something above self will inevitably result in sacrifice to some degree. This sacrifice requires people to carefully revisit the decision to serve. These times when we have to give something up, well they test our resolve to serve. This is a natural test of our core motivations.

I couldn't bear the thought of quitting. I needed to be in the smaller group that kept on going. The near-term comfort of quitting could never match the permanent comfort of accomplishment. This was one of few times in my life I could see certain ways I was different from most. Not better, but different. This notion of high-level national defense was one for which I was made. I could stick with it. There were areas I wasn't made for, but here, my motivation saw me through. I thought it was the same for Rob by the way he carried himself and by the way he talked. I was wrong. He quit right away. In this environment, most folks feel shame about quitting with their peers beside them. That's why it's very common for quitters to leave in the middle of the night, when no one can see them. In training phases when only four hours or less are granted for sleep each night, it doesn't take long for anyone to go to sleep. There's not much chance of waking them up easily either. This is the time to leave, because you won't have to face anyone. No one, that is, except the one who is on guard duty when you leave.

It was only a couple hundred yards to the barracks building we called the VW Shack. "VW" stood for voluntary withdrawal. This was the official term for quitting. Voluntary withdrawal. So in the night, the quitters would do "the duffel bag drag to the shack of shame." Invariably, they would leave their allocation of MREs behind because they would have mess hall and PX privileges immediately. Who would want constipation casserole instead of steamy hot chow from the mess hall and snacks and ice cream from the Post Exchange? A few resourceful guys learned early on to get up early, to check for empty bunks that might have MREs left behind. Extra chow could be a big help in this gut check of a program.

I don't recall the point where Rob dropped out, and it became just a part of the changing landscape, that shifting human terrain that is such a challenge in and of itself. I recall feeling surprised and disappointed. Each time a buddy dropped out, I felt a little more alone, but I had no time to linger or dwell on it. If it was someone I didn't know at all, I remember the feeling of being stronger than those who left. As insensitive as that seems, it's a pretty good survival mechanism. Their giving up became my fuel to persevere.

What does this have to do with building a team? Well, when I linked up with ol' Rob again, over a decade later, I found that my assessment of him was largely based on a nostalgic feeling of having shared experiences and times in the past. At that point, I would have felt great about having an old friend take a place on my A-Team. In fact, we once again began spending a bit of personal time together. I certainly don't see less value in a person if they are not a Green Beret, though I see that kind of faulty thinking often. In our case, Rob and I were assigned to the same unit, so there was a lot to look forward to. Much synergy was possible with our familiarity, depending on our professional approaches. That optimism was fleeting.

When we got to Kandahar, on our first deployment together, I volunteered for the big mission with the 3rd Special Forces Group (Airborne). Right away, I could see that it was a mistake to consider Rob to be a part of my personal A-Team. I know, I know, who cares whether they make my personal A-Team or not! I'm not saying that's some kind of achievement. It may not be any real achievement for anyone to be considered a part of our inner circle in life, but that doesn't make it less important for each of us to choose the right people to be shareholders in our lives. The bottom line is that I let good feelings and good intentions prevail, while clear negative indicators existed that I should have prioritized.

When I was introduced to the A-Team I would go into battle with, I had less than 72 hours to prepare for combat as a teammate. This meant that my gear needed to match theirs. Standard Operating Procedures (SOPs) in combat must be adhered to meticulously, as lives truly depend on it. These Standard Operating Procedures are developed as a team in order to function efficiently and have seamless transitions and interoperability among all members. In daylight and darkness, under intense pressure and danger, members of the team must know exactly where the ammunition is kept within personal gear. The same goes for pyrotechnic devices, communications equipment, batteries, and first aid items like tourniquets, bandages, or IV fluids. Briefings, planning sessions, and equipment preparation dominated the time available. That minimized my available time to ready my personal gear, which had been set up differently from how this team set up their gear. Basically, for Operational Detachment Alpha (A-Team) 331, I was a turd in their punchbowl.

It was late by the time I could work on my gear back at the hooch. My brothers in the Civil Affairs unit were all very eager to help me and worked hard to help me get ready. All except one. Rob lay in his bed, unwilling to help at all. In fact, he was now ignoring me and avoiding me, aside from the stern warning that the lights had better be turned off within 30 minutes. He then put a sleep mask back over his eyes and laid back down on his back, as though he were Richie Rich or Thurston Howell, III, the guy from *Gilligan's Island*. This was inconceivable, given that we were in Kandahar, Afghanistan. I thought I was watching an episode of *MASH*, the only other place I had witnessed such eccentric behavior in the Army. When the convoy lined up to roll out of the gates into Taliban country late the next night, many of my friends and peers from the Civil Affairs unit were up and out there to see me off. Rob was not.

There had been absolutely no disagreements between Rob and myself. There was nothing wrong, it seemed. He just started ignoring me and avoiding me from the moment it was determined that I was going back to an A-Team for a combat mission. This was my profession, my life, and I couldn't conceive of what the rub might be with my old army buddy. I have my suspicions by the way he used his rank to place burdens on my preparation and on those helping me. It also appeared that Rob was competing for the attention and focus of the men. Usually, envy has something to do with this behavior.

You already know what happened to me on that mission. Later, while I was still in a wheelchair from being gravely wounded, I once again faced Rob. His words are forever burned into my mind with that loud Boston accent. Rob said, "Be careful what you ask for, Stube. Nobody ever told you not to volunteer for nothin'?"

At first, I wanted to hurt him. I couldn't believe he would say that. It seemed so thoughtless, but he stuck to it. That is a sentiment more appropriate for getting stuck on a detail in the mess hall, peeling potatoes all day. It still echoes for me today: "Be careful what you ask for." I still feel sorry for him, because he obviously never shared the great and powerful feeling of patriotic service as the rest of us. What was his motivation to be there? To be in the U.S. Army? To be a commissioned officer?

This made me think back to when we were both candidates in the Special Forces' program. We both volunteered for the opportunity to try to qualify to be Green Berets. It made me recall how easily he just quit with such a great opportunity to serve in a storied capacity. Why would he just leave, when so many resources had been allocated to his opportunity to succeed? It doesn't seem like a waste of taxpayer dollars when someone gets hurt, or fails to meet standards. But to just quit? When I saw him many years later, I didn't think of any of that, but as soldiers, it matters. Why *was* he serving? Was it for something greater than himself? He openly and shamelessly expressed to me that I should not have gone to fight with our brothers for America, for freedom and safety.

Teams are fluid things because people are complicated. We must constantly reevaluate and to see how various people fit together to achieve a mission on the battlefield, in business, and life.

6

HOW TO AVOID LANDMINES AND SNIPERS

The Battlefield of Life Is Often Set
with Traps We Make

"Courage is grace under pressure."

—ERNEST HEMINGWAY

Now that you have assembled your team, it's time to perform practice sessions and dry runs to turn them into a team. As you do, you need to cut out anyone who doesn't fit, no matter how great their merits. My years of experience on Green Beret A-Teams taught me that even on the battlefield, most of the real landmines aren't actually real landmines, but are oversights, unforeseen obstacles, and personality clashes. Team training is the time to root out these landmines. Sometimes this means cutting team members who just don't fit and possibly making some substitutions.

Some guys in the Special Forces are like the description given to the character Gunny Highway (played by Clint Eastwood) in the movie *Heartbreak Ridge* when he is told some warriors need to be "sealed in a case that reads 'break glass only in the event of war!'" There are some Green Berets like that. At a certain point in my career, I guess I was even like that.

So, yeah, it almost goes without saying that Green Berets can be counted on across the board to be fit and trained for war, as tactically and technically, they are highly trained and proficient at their job. But sometimes you need more than Rambo. In general, because of the academic and performance standards required in the Special Forces, most of the guys have a great capacity for social interaction and intellectuality. But some are as close to the stereotype of an action-hero as you can get in real life.

Though these types are what you need in moments of intense action, it's important to understand the weaknesses these sorts of people carry with them. Though the mindset of someone volunteering to serve in a combat capacity involves some degree of acknowledging and accepting the risks involved, that decision does not, however, mean that each person sees that service in the same way. A warrior—or even an ad salesman or stockbroker—needs to see themselves playing that role effectively in their mind before they can do it in real life. Because Green Berets do extreme things, they need the ability to step outside themselves as they see themselves succeeding in the mission at hand despite the obstacles. But we are not all going to see ourselves the same way in these situations, and we shouldn't, as we all have different roles to play, even when we're on the same team.

So, okay, in traditional military roles, this can be pretty clear. You either want to play that role or you don't, because it's a pretty straightforward that certain Military Occupational Specialties involve doing certain sets of things. In general, the switch is either "on" or "off." A soldier has either committed to the duty and risk, or they haven't. It seems simple, but it's amazing how deep a person can go in denial. The way we see ourselves and visualize the future is pretty much how we put one foot in front of the other and continue in life. However, it is pretty common to have some faulty or wishful thinking going on even with vetted members on your team. The way others see us is often very different.

My favorite example is still the one who joins "for the college money" without serious consideration for the fact they may wind up in combat. This person has preferred to detach themselves from much of the reality they've brought on themselves. These people are often a train wreck when reality sets in and they have to face their commitments. The National Guard and the Reserves have the same kind of issues with people—maybe to a larger extent. Some of them likely get used to the paycheck while staying at home and don't let it sink in that the party could be over any day if their country needs them. Deployment can be a real circus, just watching some of them squirming.

Among Green Berets, you'll never see that. Instead, you're more likely to get serious complaints if there isn't a way to get into the action soon enough. For these guys, the self-image and idea of what they'll be doing isn't a switch that's either "on" or "off." They know that peace is not their profession, and they know whether there's a war or not, hostile fire zones and flashpoints around the world will drag them in. Most don't have to be dragged or even turned toward the action. They run toward it as soon as they hear the call to action. The switch is "on," and it stays that way.

For Green Berets, it becomes more of a question of what kind of mission we see ourselves doing as a Special Forces guy around the world. There is a set of mission types that Special Forces units are designed to address, but, within that range of missions, we all have personal preferences for what we love to do the most. Below, I've listed the major types of Special Forces missions that Green Berets wind up carrying out. Much of it can relate to civilian occupations throughout our society, and I'm sure, by reading this, you can tell what kind of mission profile you would prefer. You probably have relatable functions in your life now.

Here are the types of missions that Green Berets are made to do:

- ▶ **Unconventional Warfare (UW):** A broad spectrum of military and paramilitary operations conducted in enemy-held, enemy-controlled, or politically sensitive territory. UW includes, but is not limited to, the interrelated fields of guerilla warfare, evasion and escape, subversion, sabotage, and other operations of a low visibility, covert, or clandestine nature. Conduct a broad spectrum of military and paramilitary operations.
- ▶ **Direct Action (DA):** Either overt or covert action against an enemy force. Seize, damage, or destroy a target; capture or recover personnel or material in support of strategic/operational objectives or conventional forces.
- ▶ **Special Reconnaissance (SR):** Special Forces teams infiltrate behind enemy lines to provide the theater commander with

intelligence on the enemy or to gather information on the terrain, local populace, and so forth of an area. Verify, through observation or other collection methods, information concerning enemy capabilities, intentions, and activities in support of strategic/operational objectives or conventional forces.

▶ **Foreign Internal Defense (FID):** FID operations are designed to help friendly developing nations by working with host country military and police forces to improve their technical skills, understanding of human rights issues, and to help with humanitarian and civic action projects. FID missions assist another government in any action program taken to free and protect its society from subversion, lawlessness, and insurgency.

▶ **Counter Terrorism (CT):** Offensive measures taken to prevent, deter, and respond to terrorism. Preempt or resolve terrorist incidents. Interagency activity using highly specialized capabilities.

▶ **Psychological Operations (PSYOP):** Induce or reinforce foreign attitudes and behavior favorable to U.S. objectives. Influence emotions, motives, and behavior of foreign governments, organizations, groups, and individuals.

▶ **Civil Affairs (CA):** Establish, maintain, influence, or exploit relations among military forces, civil authorities, and civilian populations to facilitate military operations.

▶ **Coalition Warfare/Support:** Ensures the ability of a wide variety of foreign troops to work together effectively in a wide variety of military exercises or operations such as Operation Desert Storm. Draws upon the SOF soldier's maturity, military skills, language skills, and cultural awareness.

▶ **Humanitarian and Civic Action (HCA):** SOF soldiers' diversified military skills, language capabilities, and cultural training makes them a natural choice for supporting humanitarian and civic action operations.

▶ **Other Individual Missions:** Besides the individual skills of operations and intelligence, communications, medical aid, engineering, and weapons, each Special Forces soldier is taught to train, advise, and assist host-nation military or paramilitary forces. Special Forces soldiers are highly skilled operators, trainers, and teachers. Area-oriented, these soldiers are specially trained in their area's native language and culture.

Within these types of missions, each person is likely to have a sweet spot. The problem for an A-Team can come when one or more team members don't relate to the mission at hand and it doesn't fit what they ever imagined doing as a Green Beret. It's enough to leave someone feeling temporarily unfulfilled. People are different. Some love sneaky ninja stuff. Some love cultural dynamics and winning hearts and minds. Others love putting puzzles together and figuring out solutions to bigger problems. While one may really want the heroic action of rescuing good guys and shooting bad guys, another may be uniquely driven to help people live better lives in lesser-developed areas. Some want to teach, and others would rather watch from a distance and report with strategic focus.

While each special skill area within the career field of the Green Beret brings unique considerations to team operations, they are all unified on the team to contribute collectively to the specific mission accomplishment. Weapons, communications, engineers, and medical sergeants all get on board for the big win. Many times, I was not a medic until something went wrong. That means I had to get comfortable with being a shooter or whatever else was called for in the effort. Here comes the rub in the selection process for a mission: Within the team, you'll rarely, if ever, find someone who is against doing whatever must be done to support teammates and the mission at hand. That is, until someone finds they are in a role that doesn't match their personal image of what a Green Beret should be doing.

This is why it's critical to foresee how different personalities will fit with every mission and to cut team members or add them as necessary. Cutting someone from the A-Team (or not selecting them in the first place) is usually due to personal factors or problems at the time, unless it has to do with an obvious inability to assimilate to the current role required. The former can happen to anyone, and it does. The latter, however, usually occurs with a caveman type of person.

This Rambo-variety guy just wants to shoot bad guys. That's it. That's what he came for. It's what he was born to do. This guy will likely say something like, "This is no SF mission!" The thing is it is usually an SF mission—just not one he is wired to do. Actually, direct action is not the center of the universe for a Green Beret. But a mouth-breather with a primitive mindset will resent the thought of doing anything less than killing bad guys. This kind of guy was perhaps my biggest disappointment in the Special Forces, but you just can't get a big enough group of guys to fit the Green Beret profile without having a few knuckle-draggers in the bunch.

It was always a liability to have someone on the team who felt no compassion or anything warm for members of our host nation. This seemed unreasonable to me and beckoned thoughts of the classic "ugly American." It's hard to contribute to a helpful dynamic when you refer to everyone around you as "savages." More than once, these coarse individuals had to be removed from, or not selected for, teams that would have contact with the locals in helpful efforts.

In Bosnia and Kosovo for most of the 1990s, many facets of peacekeeping became a focus for the Special Forces. In many of these roles, it was necessary to perform liaison functions, to maintain personal contact with local leaders, and more. It has always been important to ascertain local sentiments and to provide an honest assessment of what's really going on in order for U.S. foreign policy efforts to succeed.

This was an important example of needing Special Forces skills to negotiate tricky and dangerous places and situations, but not to shoot unless absolutely necessary. Millions of landmines were in the ground, and smaller ones were left for kids in order to arouse their curiosity and entice them to play with them. Genocide and mass killing had been underway for years, and the effects of civil war were not over. Violence knocked on the door to threaten each day, and it seemed like new threats to our own safety evolved routinely.

The ability to stabilize the region depended on being able to make good assessments where diplomats just weren't safe to hang out. That meant we would need to be just warrior enough to get in and exist in not-so-safe areas, while being just statesmen or diplomatic enough to build relationships and establish roads forward in a broken country.

To gain access and placement meant that we could facilitate necessary support for local and regional concerns in post-war rebuilding. All the while, we needed to keep our ear to the ground and to be prepared for the violent stuff at any moment. It was unique to maintain combat readiness while keeping a relaxed and non-threatening appearance. From aspects of that work, I can identify with what our law-enforcement officers face today.

The worst thing that could happen in some cases would be to break hard-earned rapport with local entities. This is why it became necessary to make cuts and restrictions for Rambo's participation in these efforts. If you couldn't show respect or even kindness toward the people we were there to assist, then you were a liability. While this person was not really common, we had to keep a few guys in their "break glass in the event of war" cases. I was always disappointed by that, because my own vision of Green Berets had been based on their historic application of teaching and winning hearts and minds, all the while being ultimate combat warriors in case something went wrong. Fighting should be seen as the downside. Almost anything else is a blessing. To me, we had to cut people who were tougher than they were smart or compassionate.

Don't Let Team Changes Harm Your Focus

As you cut and shape a team, you'll soon find that you must keep it going in the right direction, as it is easy to lose focus. Keeping the team headed toward the goal means you need to define the goals clearly and to stick to them as you get the team in step. It also means making tough decisions about the mission and team. These will test you and your convictions. Soon, you'll find out that when it costs you something to be honest about your beliefs, you'll know just how much you believe in your dreams—even if they are nothing but fantasies. Then your vision, even your integrity, will be on the line as it must be as you lead or work within this new team.

That said, I pity anyone who has never felt what it's like to be part of a team that's hitting on all cylinders. I don't care whether it is a Special Ops team or a weekend softball team; it feels powerful to have synergy with other people in a common pursuit. It's even better when you're winning.

So, okay, let's step back a second and acknowledge that we love a great team. Professional and collegiate sports are a cornerstone of American culture for an important reason. We admire a team that has cohesion and that can perform under pressure. What we admire from afar is achievable in our own lives. From choosing who will be on your team, to maintaining progress as a team, to staying in step through victory and defeat, it all relies on a few things that you can have some control over.

Whether it's a sniper, a mine, or a personality that doesn't fit, it is best to keep that stuff outside your own perimeter. Assessment and selection help you keep clear of enemies within. The person may not actually be an enemy, but the conditions they create will be. You shouldn't automatically eject or exclude people who aren't outwardly friendly, but if tactful or even strong suggestion doesn't improve someone's bad attitude, then anywhere else would be a better place for them.

In any unit, and in any operation, safety is one of the few things that everyone must take part in regardless of rank. Safety is *everyone's* responsibility. Before the prevalence of terrorism, basic operational safety was the impetus for the concept we know as "see something, say something." Each of us is required to speak up when we see something that isn't safe. When someone can get hurt, and resources can be lost. It's not an appropriate course of action to just watch it unfold and then explain how it happened later as an eyewitness. I like to take our active engagement beyond safety, to expand and deepen involvement in all things "team." The bottom line is to let it begin with you. Yes, safety first! But let's show that kind of ownership and concern with everything we do.

The Unappreciated Landmine

Invariably, some feel unappreciated, which can be simply from a lack of communication. Silence is deadly to a team. It always helps to make an effort to create positive communication whenever possible. Recognizing assets that individuals bring to the team is necessary; allow people to see their value on the team clearly. It is fundamental to pool collective assets in the creation of a winning team. But many leaders fail to motivate others by withholding compliments. While external validation is not the most important thing among intrinsically motivated people, there seems to be one or two on every team who just can't get by without it. If their validation is left unattended, these folks can harbor resentment that may become problematic. They might not be serving in the best interests of the team, at that point, but it's easy to prevent resentment through active communication.

In the effort to recognize and utilize team assets, don't stop short. Never be satisfied simply because you have good people and they fall in line. They may even be the best at what they do, but sometimes they can't see or don't look outside the lines they have always followed. Leaders can sometimes help them find improved and varied applications of their talents. Vince Lombardi is one of the most celebrated coaches of all time. Part of what made him so effective was the way he tuned in to the specific strengths and capabilities of each player and pursued non-traditional ways for each player to apply those strengths. He really knew how to get outside the box to put pieces of the puzzle together in superior and unconventional ways. It was a winning recipe that required very personal attention to each team member. In contrast, failure to tailor your team's strengths and weaknesses to the objectives at hand is to simply waste resources. This proves to be a consistent way to drop the ball before you even take possession of it. You don't have to be Vince Lombardi to pay close attention to team assets and put them to work.

"Loyalty" and "integrity" are two watchwords held in high regard for team development. They are wonderful characteristics to enjoy, and they already exist in many people. Still, the absence of these things is catastrophic. A cascade of negative events tends to occur in an environment bereft of loyalty and integrity. Many will even choose not to participate on such a team.

It seems some folks just have these attributes, but how do we capture it for the benefit of the overall team, and for people who haven't caught the bug yet? This is one of the more difficult things to do. Developing loyalty and integrity is a personal and intimate affair. A good team becomes much like a family—they might be slightly dysfunctional at times, but they love each other, so the mission gets done.

The danger in this is this team bond can be a false motivator. If they are doing the mission because of their relationships with each other and not because they believe in the mission, then you are setting yourself up to fail. Now, some say false motivation is better than no motivation, but I don't think so. False motivation just can't survive when a person's convictions are tested. The lack of true motivation cannot sustain adversity. We need to be prepared to face challenges and problems and to be able to see them through. We need to win, and it needs to be in a way that overcomes adversity and fosters team unity—this means fighting with honor for things we can all agree are good.

Now, some commercials mock corporate motivation efforts. This is because so many organizational cheerleaders out there are simply surrogates and not truly organic to the team. Their efforts fall flat. Often, a motivational speaker is just repeating material that is not specific to the audience. (Motivational speakers are people who make money pumping sunshine into our lower posteriors. They pump people up, but their hot air is gone fast.) There are real reasons why you probably can't even imagine a motivational speaker trying to get a Special Forces team going—those guys would eat the speaker on the spot.

Other times, we are fed motivational tunes by someone in the organization who has been tapped by higher ups to get the team going. This does happen in the Army, even in the Special Forces. Still, the selection of this person needs to be done thoughtfully. If this person hasn't walked in the boots of the men and women to whom they are speaking, then they won't be respected—and they won't even know *how* to talk to the team. If the person chosen to carry the message doesn't feel personally invested, or if they just don't relate and connect with people well, then it falls flat; it feels like someone is up there saying this stuff because they have to, and they are simply being paid to "wave the flag." Likewise, if there is any element of self-preservation or self-promotion in the message, then they will lose their audience, big or small. The most important thing in any organized effort to develop motivation, loyalty, and integrity is that the person presenting it must have motivation, loyalty, and integrity. Anything less is a detectable fraud. There's no substitute for genuine feelings and real identity for someone who walks the walk.

An example like that pays dividends for any team, but the ability to communicate such blessings of mindset and orientation may prove necessary to convert members who may be short on maturity, experience, or belief. I find similarities between these pursuits and religion. In fact, I believe these concepts can come easier for people of faith who are already tuned in to serving something above themselves. We can all spot a selfless team player, a true believer. Team building can enhance a person's spiritual life, and vice versa, in my opinion. They go hand in hand. It's a good understanding to have. A lack of motivation, belief, or conviction can cause critical failure. Besides, it feels so good and works so well when everyone is "leaning forward in the foxhole" together, believing in what they are doing.

How to See Problems Coming

Threats, obstacles, and opposition are things we should be planning for, but we often don't. If we can identify these things in advance, we certainly want to. In life, one thing that takes up too much space is excuses. I'm almost certain that every one of us winds up blaming things that impede our progress or torpedo our plans. These are things we never expected because they are seldom organic to the plan itself. They come from somewhere else while we are busy looking on the bright side. What often happens is our view of success is unfettered by reality. Reality, though, has a way of suddenly interfering anyway. This is why we need to plan for the worst-case scenario, and to stop expecting the best case to prevail. It won't.

The best of plans could never eliminate the bad intentions of Mr. Murphy, but good planning can mitigate many problems, both predictable and unforeseen. In the Special Forces, we have developed generations' worth of perspective on how to plan both offensively and defensively when the world around us is trying to take us down. Let's take a look at some of the concepts that are successful in preparing for anything, and you'll see that they can apply to anything in front of you. It's true that the best plans only remain intact until the first bullet is fired, or that, as Mike Tyson said, "Everybody has a plan till they get hit in the mouth." But that doesn't mean we can't prepare in ways to prolong or even to prevent such problems.

Here is how to predict and avoid obstacles to our success.

Two acronyms are used in a detailed tactical approach to military missions:

▶ **METT-TC** (**M**–mission, **E**–enemy, **T**–terrain and weather, **T**–troops, **T**–time available, **C**–civilian considerations)
▶ **OCOKA** (**O**–observations and fields of fire, **C**–cover and concealment, **O**–obstacles, **K**–key or decisive terrain, **A**–avenues of approach.)

These two short lists give us a solid range of considerations in our assessment and preparation for objectives we face. While they are designed for military missions, I'm sure you will agree that they have absolute parallels in everyday life.

METT-TC gets us focused on the basic set of resources we are working with. It forces us to take inventory and to create a realistic starting point for what is to be accomplished. One of the greatest competencies is a developed ability to recognize, quantify, and use available resources for the accomplishment of any objective. METT-TC sets us up for success in that way.

M Is for Mission

"Mission" is a word used heavily in a military context, but it is also used in significant ways to define the goals of any company, organization, or individual. Because of the often-grave nature of a military mission, it carries a special meaning for me and continues to be a defining word for my status and activity at any time. If not, then I should be reconsidering my focus and direction. I believe the word "mission" assigns importance and infers commitment. I like it when I hear people use that word, because it usually means they take things seriously. Although "mission" has a certain gravity attached to it, the use of the word demands a thorough look at what the true objectives are, and, especially, what the primary intent is. Intent is the biggest concern in the planning and execution of any mission. That is often the single biggest responsibility of commanders and leaders everywhere. On an A-Team, the detachment commander is the only officer on the team. He is forever herding lions and managing good-idea fairies in his efforts to maintain mindfulness of, and adherence to, the actual intent of the mission at hand. Without this adherence to mission, our great ideas and our great conceptions of ourselves would have us going in some other direction, or many directions at once, and then we wouldn't accomplish anything.

Whether we are dealing with true Type-A personalities, like those on an A-Team, or not, the quality people we engage with will have much to contribute. But be careful, as when solutions are sought, great ideas can inadvertently steer us away from our original mission. We can feel so good about our innovative ideas that we can forget about constraints, restraints, and other considerations for making the mission a success. Compliance with the original intent is harder than it seems, and it gets harder with high-quality, forward-thinking contributors on the team. It takes a detached sort of objectivity to keep an eye on the intent and to keep the mission on course.

Great ideas and serious approaches to certain challenging elements of any plan can absorb the greater focus and become a distraction. Certain elements of a plan can become monsters of intense focus and effort. During these times, it's necessary to refer to the M in METT-TC and have someone in charge of safeguarding the original mission at hand. It's embarrassing to present an intricate and complex plan that has taken untold hours to complete, and then to find that it doesn't even satisfy the original intent. We get distracted. It happens. This is a way to stay on top of it.

E Is for Enemy

I know; "enemy" is a strong word. In the military context, it is self-explanatory. In other applications, it may seem as if we've gone overboard. I would argue that if something requires effort to achieve, then resistance in some form must be present. That resistance is the enemy, whether it is a natural barrier to success, an opposing team, or any form of competitor. Don't forget that with the wrong focus, attitude, or activity, we can be our own worst enemy without any help at all from outside forces.

Knowing yourself is important, yes. But knowing your enemy is of equal concern. I don't think it's realistic to claim any efficacy without a well-grounded and working knowledge of our resistance. Whether we face an opposing ideology or tactic, we are foolish to think we have a real strategy without understanding what the opposition brings to the table. What is their belief and motivation? What places them at odds with us? What are the commonalities and differences between them and us? Why do they think they are right? Why do they think we are wrong? How do they view their own strengths versus ours?

The enemy might be competition in business, it might be an opposing sports team, it might be cancer, or it might be an opposing political view. To defeat it, we must understand it just as we must understand ourselves.

We might see ourselves as the good guys and see the opposition as the bad guys. But, because we perceive the others to be bad, that does not reduce the need to understand their ideology and motivation. In fact, we can't begin to compare or compete with them without understanding the differences and the commonalities.

An example I see often is our reaction to media. So often, when we see or hear something we are opposed to, we change the station or tune it out. We don't listen to the things and people with whom we disagree. It's almost as if we feel that listening or watching is somehow approving of the message. It is not. Not only do our beliefs need to be well founded in relation to all that exists, but we cannot effectively represent our position if we don't understand what makes it the same or different from opposing views or opinions.

John Stuart Mill, in his book *On Liberty* (1859), outlined the need to challenge our convictions by saying:

> First, if any opinion is compelled to silence, that opinion may, for all we can certainly know, be true. To deny this is to assume our own infallibility.

Secondly, though the silenced opinion is an error, it may, and very well commonly does, contain a portion of the truth; and since the general or prevailing opinion on any object is rarely or never the whole truth, it is only by the collision of adverse opinions that the remainder of the truth has any chance of being supplied.

Thirdly, even if the received opinion is not only true, but the whole truth; unless it is suffered to be, and actually is, vigorously and earnestly contested, it will, by most of those who receive it, be held in the manner of prejudice, with little comprehension or feeling of its rational grounds.

From another perspective, the importance of knowing your enemy was summed up well in Matthew 10:16 of the King James Bible: "Behold, I send you forth as sheep in the midst of wolves: be ye therefore wise as serpents, and harmless as doves." I view this scripture to mean that gaining wisdom through knowledge of the enemy is imperative to surviving engagements with them. It tells me to open my eyes and ears to the things I don't agree with or like, even to evil things, while maintaining my own innocence, or rightful position. To know the difference requires exposure to stuff I don't like, but I tune in to avoid being ignorant; after all, I might be wrong.

This is of particular interest when success, or even your very survival, is threatened by such opposition. The survival I speak of could be anything from your mortal life to the existence of your business or the success or failure of teams and respective missions in your life. If ministry means anything in your life, or you think promoting and sharing what you believe is good for people, then you must know the difference and live in the real world or no one will put stock in you. Credibility and context do matter.

Pay attention to the "E for Enemy" so it doesn't easily have its way with you and your good intentions. Failure to address opposition or resistance is a recipe for preventable disaster.

T Is for Terrain and Weather

While this may simply apply to environmental factors for troops in the field, to us it should mean much more in a broader sense. I translate it as human terrain and operational environment. This can remind us to take a good look at the overall dynamics of human factors, as well as anything that affects the climate or attitude we will be exposed to. Politics may be at hand, religion may be a prevalent factor, nepotism may dominate, or cliques could complicate or even destroy your team.

While we may have a more complex approach to the "T in METT-TC" than the typical grunt, we still need to use this reminder to assess the basic natural and man-made elements of the area we'll be functioning in. It goes without saying that the weather is one of the things that needs consideration in planning. The terrain and weather deserve some research, insight, and forethought. Some of the cultural implications can be showstoppers, or, at least, barriers that deserve attention. They can also create support, power, and influence for your cause. You'll need to use the "T" to distinguish the difference and be prepared.

The Next T Is for Troops

Who are the troops? Who do you have active in your effort? This is where you must list the people who are organic to your team, and, in many cases, additional folks in various support roles. Whether it is for the assignment of talents to respective tasks, distribution of resources, or merely for accountability of personnel, this "T" is fundamental to all things "team." Don't forget anyone.

The Last T Is for Time Available

Tracking multiple schedules in order to create an overall timeline for success happens for most things we do. No one wants to be late to the game, and failing to meet deadlines is a sure way to sink your own effort. Time seems like the simplest facet of planning for mission success. Deadlines, arrivals, departures, and timelines themselves are straightforward, but they become complicated when each person involved may have different personal and professional schedules or transportation considerations, with varying time available for the objective at hand. Use this last "T" for reference in getting synced up as a team. This is where you will identify and utilize available time needed as a team, versus time needed for individual tasks. It is often hard to create slots for mandatory team time or maximum participation, but assessing the time available is the only way to get it done for the sake of information dissemination, planning efforts, votes, rehearsals, and much more. Everything takes time. If you don't plan for it, you will most likely run out of it.

C Is for Civilian Considerations

In military applications, this applies to anyone not in the military. My drill sergeant had always warned us to stay away from those dirty, nasty civilians! Good thing that's not what it means here. Easily enough for these purposes, civilian considerations would pertain to anyone not directly involved or engaged in the effort at hand. Usually, we must share space and certain resources with others in society. The "C" in METT-TC is where we stop to consider how sharing space and resources with others not involved could affect us. It's also the time to take a good look at how we might impact them. This one can get really sticky and create accountable situations and even litigation. Evaluate these considerations carefully. Have a plan for interaction with uninvolved or uninterested parties. Communicate that plan well throughout the entire team. Don't allow innocent bystanders to be affected adversely, and prevent them from having adverse effects on your success. Civilian considerations aren't always a concern, but when they come into play, they deserve your full attention.

Aside from these acronyms as guides to follow, I would add that there was always an implied directive in place in the Army for individual conduct. It echoes in my head even now: "Be in the right place, at the right time, in the right uniform, with the right equipment and the right attitude." Those standards create discomfort at first, but you'll soon find that showing up is half the battle.

The same thing exists in many places, I suppose, but it was spoken so often by so many in the Army that it still stays with me. Oh, yeah, and it was always punishable if you came up short. Maybe that's part of why I remember it so well. My guess is that I'm not alone, and that the ways the military engenders structure, standards, and discipline is a big reason many employers seek veterans. They are team players. I hope we, as veterans, continue to live up to that and to the reputation of American warriors using what we have learned to the benefit of our families, communities, and country.

Another simple guide we always used for consideration in planning and approach to operations was the acronym OCOKA. This one digs in a bit more in a tactical sense, but it still promotes better awareness of factors working for you and against you in any effort. Without applying specific considerations like this, the odds are good that we will overlook too much. If we choose simply to follow our gut instincts and experience, we are seldom keen to details that are different than in previous experiences. Never get too smart to use reference, particularly when others are counting on you.

OCOKA is one acronym that no combat unit would ever want to proceed without. Women and men in the outdoors can surely benefit from this kind of assessment tool on their adventures too. I actually see unlimited application in it for life in general. See if you agree. As you read over these guides for planning considerations and points of awareness, keep in mind that if these are key considerations from your own perspective, then they are also important to consider from the perspective of your opposition or competition. Effectively, you would want to go over it once for "us" and once for "them." This can more than double your understanding of the operational environment and boost overall preparedness.

O Is for Observation and Fields of Fire

Oversight, supervision, and control rely heavily on visibility or transparency. While the military context pertains to the ability to see and maintain effective weapons coverage over a given area, or to watch for enemy movement, I like to think of observation in a more general way. Gaining and maintaining a view over your operational area is important. Simplified, it's just like playing chess. I always say that a good leader can't afford to get mired in a low-level task. If they do, then they lose the greater view of the entire area of responsibility. The "catwalk" is the reference I like to make for staying above the moving parts to maintain the greater view for accuracy in command and control issues. In complex operations with multiple involved areas, it becomes necessary to utilize the visibility of others with differing vantage points. Good communication helps to paint the overall picture for a leader who needs to stay on that proverbial catwalk when they can't see it with their own eyes.

Being able to observe certain areas becomes critical in being able to employ resources in support of current objectives.

C Is for Cover and Concealment

While these two words may sound similar, to a soldier, there is a critical difference. "Cover" will stop bullets, but "concealment" won't! In general, application of these terms, I think of the difference between what I want others to see, and what needs to be reserved for the team only. Sometimes we have intellectual property that needs to be protected. Sometimes how we do things is something we'd like to keep to ourselves. Other times, there is a presentation to be made and seen with certain support functions at play that don't need to be seen at all. This is where it helps to analyze the operational area for possible cover and concealment to use in support of your objectives. Your analysis of cover and concealment is not complete until you also ascertain how any opposition might remain hidden or protected in efforts that work against you.

O Is for Obstacles

The presence of obstacles is a universal thing and needs no translation. Obstacles slow things down, create damage, or may even cause complete failure. At a minimum, they are a distraction. Most obstacles are observable and predictable, but some are not. Being prepared requires a look at what can get in the way, both seen and unseen. Making specific preparations for known obstacles is the easier part, as long as we take the time to identify and list the obstacles. Planning to overcome unknown obstacles as a set of contingencies takes more consideration, forethought, and experience.

Along with the drawbacks that obstacles bring to the home team, there can certainly be advantages in using existing ones or created barriers to impede the progress of adversaries. This is not to say that sabotage is called for, or even acceptable. However, if we have to deal with obstacles, then so do they, right? Our mindfulness can allow for better outcomes and less excuses. It's about using available resources and recognizing obstacles that can turn out to be one and the same, depending on which side you're on.

K Is for Key or Decisive Terrain

The hilltop we fought for in Afghanistan, called Sperwan Ghar, was key or decisive terrain. To look at the danger and the cost involved with fighting for that high ground is to illuminate what a difference key terrain makes. We needed that hilltop to maintain better observation and control of the area, just like how the Union Army needed that little ridge called "Cemetery Ridge" just outside Gettysburg to get the upper hand with invading Confederate troops in the American Civil War.

This is a detail that affects only the people who live on Earth. There are typically good places and lesser places for everything we do. The object is to pick the best place or places for what our plans involve. Whether we are looking for a place to occupy as a stationary presence, or a route to use in movement, it winds up being very important to pick a place that will support it without creating hardships. This might be the best place for the headquarters of your business, for distribution centers, and more.

More so, we want to select places that make everything easier. The terrain you occupy or negotiate can become the most difficult aspect of operations. It can also serve to make it easier. In every way possible, we need to assess how the given terrain will impact us. The results can make great difference in our effectiveness, and even our morale.

A Stands for Avenues of Approach

For military purposes, a unit always needs to be mindful of how the enemy might be able to approach and how quickly. Avenues work both ways, so it makes good sense to factor them into our plans. How we gain access to the rest of the world matters. How we deliver, as well as how we receive, matters. For all of us, this is constantly evolving. An avenue of approach can pertain to communication, physical deliveries, travel, and movement of any kind. Knowing the ways to reach other places and people matters. The way they can reach you is equally important. Do your homework so you are aware of all avenues that exist both ways. Understand the nature of more and less efficient avenues for all things required and intended by the plan you wish to execute. Some of this, in our modern day, requires a very tech-savvy look. Rapid modernization of communication and transportation means has created a need for timely and innovative assessments for good planning. Technological advantages are present for those paying attention and seeking the latest information. The avenues available for the movement of communications, people, and resources will always be critical to any plan.

Recognizing the potential of landmines and snipers is something we all need to do, but we forget so much each day. It helps to have a system and a plan to address these concerns fully on the front end. If we are only reactive, instead of proactive, these things will deal with us, rather than us dealing with them. Being able to avert both internal and external enemies and obstacles takes mindfulness and planning. Implementing a system that you can refer to and repeat is necessary for consistency and for a thorough approach. Failing to plan is planning to fail.

Next comes learning to communicate effectively.

Greg Stube retired from the U.S. Army in June 2011, shown here at the Airborne and Special Operations Museum in Fayetteville, NC. He spent nineteen of his twenty-three years in the U.S. Army serving as a Green Beret on Special Forces' A-Teams.

Stube enjoys a light moment in war-torn Bosnia in 1998 where he helped to pull people who'd been in a civil war back together. Green Beret A-Teams do a lot more than the fast and specific missions we see Special Forces' soldiers do in movies. Green Berets are also first responders who bring hope back to foreign peoples.

(*Top*) Stube, like the rest of the A-Team he was on at the time, made due with limited training facilities in the Balkans. (*Bottom*) This is a deep moment of reflection before the mission that would become known as the battle for Sperwan Ghar in the Panjwayi district in Kandahar Province, Afghanistan. Scenes repeat themselves as commanders and chaplains prepare troops for whatever is awaiting them on a mission.

(*Top*) This is Riley Stephens, a Green Beret, who Stube actually deemed NTR (Never to Return), which is part of the reason Riley was booted out of training. But Stephens did return after Stube was no longer cadre at the John F. Kennedy Special Warfare Center and School. He became a medic and would later save Stube's life. Stephens would later be killed in action. (*Bottom*) A haunting but happy memory of two of Greg's heroic teammates in war. Neither of the Green Berets shown here, Riley and Bill, survived Afghanistan. They are among many heroes we've lost since September 11, 2001.

Stube's father had said, "If I can wind up in Arlington, my life will have been worth something!" Now Chief Stube is in Arlington. (*Inset*) While still on active duty, Stube says goodbye to his dad in Arlington National Cemetery.

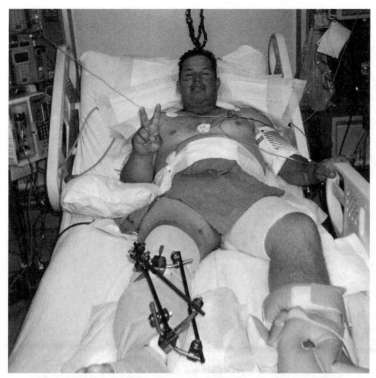

In August 2006, Stube was blown up, shot, and badly burned during Operation Medusa, a battle for Sperwan Ghar in the Panjwayi district in Kandahar Province, Afghanistan, that involved over 1,000 Taliban fighters. He would spend a year in the hospital recovering.

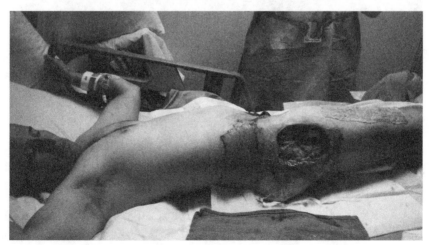

A piece of shrapnel the size of a small plate had gone right through Stube.

Colonel Andy Milani presents the Bronze Star to Stube.

(*Top*) After recovering from his wounds, Stube would begin helping other soldiers wounded in battle, first officially for the Green Berets, and later as a professional speaker. (*Bottom*) Stube continues to speak professionally to bring the values and leadership strategies he learned as a Green Beret to the rest of America. Shown behind him is General David Petraeus.

Stube with his son, Gregory, his biggest reason for surviving and coming home.

PART THREE
ACHIEVING THE MISSION

"The best executive is the one who has sense enough to pick good men to do what he wants done, and self-restraint enough to keep from meddling with them while they do it."

—THEODORE ROOSEVELT

7

NO COMMUNICATION, NO TEAM

If You Don't Talk to a Team Member, They Will Think the Worst

"When people talk, listen completely."

—ERNEST HEMINGWAY

If an A-Team loses communications, they might die. If a business team loses communication after an internal breakdown, for example, their competitors will destroy them. To make a team work, there must be open channels of communication up and down the chain of command. Many bosses say their door is always open, but only a few actually understand what that means. Within the inner dynamics of a real A-Team is a clear example that shows precisely what this means. Open communication is critical to achieve the mission, to find the best solutions, and to keep everyone on board. If you want to piss someone off, all you have to do is stop talking to them. If you do that, they'll form all kinds of opinions and dissension against you. If that happens, your team will fall apart. Also, without proper communication, creative minds can send the mission outside of its constraints and restraints, which means the plan won't accomplish the mission. To avoid these pitfalls, a Green Beret A-Team has formed a very unique culture I'll explain here.

As we build A-Teams and get them working toward objectives, it is important not to fall prey to the sometimes-popular mindsets that engender the perception that leaders don't care about those under them. I've seen the toll this takes on leaders whom I'd previously thought unaffected by my welfare and the others on the team. It's destructive and polarizing to create a perceived distance like that between any elements or members of a team, from top to bottom. The hard part is not getting as much communication as we want or access to higher-level concerns. While it's good to seek involvement and responsibility, it is also necessary to understand that our leaders often have concerns and considerations that we are shielded from. We can't see everything from our position, and sometimes we assume the worst. Negativity like this should be avoided at all costs; a good way to offset it is to vow to support your leaders in any way possible each day. Take some of the weight of daily minutia off them, if you can. They may need greater focus on important details that impact your own role and the success of the team. Through your efforts, you may also earn greater access and placement that will help you achieve better qualifications and insight for how to be promoted to positions of higher responsibility. Serving your team and its leaders is truly organic to answering the call. When times get tough, you'll want that kind of trust and mutual reliance. Let it begin with you.

A great way to foster an environment of full participation and information sharing is to involve everyone in the planning process. If it isn't practical or possible to have all present during planning sessions, then rapid information dissemination should be made a priority. Don't forget that attitudes go south when people are treated like they don't matter. No communication, no team.

Morale and confidence aren't the only things at stake when information dissemination is not practiced. Too often, we are represented or misrepresented by individuals who are members of the team but who don't have complete or accurate information. This will then affect the morale of the team.

If there is no confidential or classified information in play, then avoid weak links by sharing everything in a timely manner. Information is power, and if we don't share it with members of the team, then the perception can quickly grow that either the leadership thinks too highly of itself or they don't think enough of anyone else. It's unfortunate when a leader or team representative holds onto information they've been made privy to, only to share it with a certain circle of friends, or not at all. Illegitimately deriving a sense of privilege or power from holding information that truly belongs to the whole team is wrong. Possessing and hiding that special "globe of knowledge" is not conducive to your own reputation and can kill morale for others. With teammates like that, who needs a sniper? No communication, no team.

An unfortunate element on many teams is the development of cliques. While it is normal and natural for certain people to gravitate toward one another due to certain commonalities or shared perspectives, it can become harmful to the team and to progress itself when such social groupings create internal divisions. These social dynamics can cause professional problems with planning, execution, and information sharing. Communication is at the core of the issue. By all means, pick your own friends, but don't act like kids on the playground. Make the effort to see full value in everyone and to avoid all preferential treatment in the workplace. Treating one person better than others leads to bad impressions, bad ideas, and bad feelings. Particularly in a leadership role, leave the buddy-buddy stuff alone. Fraternization fosters the mishandling and misallocation of communication and information itself. It also quashes the notion of fairness on any team. Once you've gone down the road of picking favorites and having unprofessional relationships within a team, you'll have a dysfunctional team. Suddenly, you'll be looking at a communication failure that goes both ways. No communication, no team.

Ways of avoiding failures in communication can be incorporated into routine procedures. One good way to ensure solid information dissemination is to involve and engage everyone in the first place. Adopting a group approach, whenever possible, will not only utilize the full talent pool you have working with you, but it offers full participation, investment, and empowerment to every team member. Planning, updates, and after-action reviews can involve everyone and wind up being more complete with comprehensive participation. I like to think of it as a plan to utilize and engage the whole team before, during, and after.

Before any actions or activities get underway, a plan has to be devised on some level or to some degree. We almost certainly gain more "buy in" and confident participation from everyone by making them a part of it. The same can be said for checking in with team members during activities, when possible, and listening to their opinion of how things are going. Changing and improving on the fly is a dynamic that requires active input from the "troops on the ground." When they know their input matters, just watch how much they put into what they are doing.

People want to feel respected and credible in what they do, and it makes us all feel better to be viewed as a contributor, not a self-propelled sandbag. After performing actions as a team, it pays to collect the impressions of anyone willing to contribute to an assessment of what went down. It keeps the same mistakes from happening over and over and streamlines the process for the future. Having to re-invent the wheel each time is not the way to win. This improvement process collectively prepares the team to begin again with ever-increasing optimism and identity.

The continuum of operations in our lives includes everything: active times, down times, and times we've either heard that something is coming up, or when we're already in planning. Don't try to engage as a team simply because it's time to perform. Any sports team will tell you that the off-season practices really matter. In fact, a lot of what makes a team strong and functional happens off the field.

When I was cadre for the Special Operations Preparation Course after 9/11, I pushed for off-duty team activities. It matters what you do all the time as a team. Keeping that in mind, it pays to have an idea of ways to foster team development throughout all phases and levels of activity. What follows is a look at the three major timeframes that make up our lives, in terms of the actions and events that we relate to.

Before anything begins, making a plan is everything. It's been said that failing to plan is planning to fail. Good planning sets up the potential for successful actions. One of many leadership challenges is to ensure proper understanding of the vision and the mission among all members of the team. If certain members are isolated from or not included in the planning process, it limits their engagement, their investment, and maybe even their identity and overall understanding of things. Get everyone involved.

An extreme example of getting everyone involved and keeping them engaged is one that I learned as a Special Forces medical sergeant:

To enhance the survival and outcome of a patient, keep them engaged and involved. If they are in trouble, you can keep them in better shape mentally by allowing them to assist in some way with their own care. Sometimes holding a splint or bandage in place or squeezing on their own IV bag gives a patient a better image of his or her own outcome because they're having a hand in it. Further, if a patient could still function, it always made sense to keep them in the fight somehow. There's always something we can do. Keeping a teammate engaged and active is the best way not to lose them on any level.

As the medic, I employed these concepts to conserve the fighting strength of my team and the well-being of all involved. As a multisystem combat trauma casualty, I employed them to stay alive and fight off shock. Those lessons and experiences went a long way in shaping my ideas for keeping everyone possible "in the fight." I had no idea that I'd be able to use this concept so much more often off the battlefield, even at home, than I ever did in combat. You can too, and I hope you will.

The planning process can make us all feel useful and even smart. Everyone has something to contribute, and this isn't some fluffy "everyone's a winner" kind of psychobabble. During planning efforts and course of action development, I absolutely love observing the potential that diversity unleashes for a team. Watching a variety of skill sets, cultures, mindsets, educations, and more coming together to raise the common denominator for success is one of my favorite things. We see this collaboration portrayed so often in the casts of popular television shows, but do we realize that we have the same possibilities around us each day? Are we turning away from perceived differences to capture and utilize commonality in purpose, direction, and motivation? The planning process is a wonderful opportunity to see how our differences can provide solutions to problems we haven't overcome yet. Life gets pretty boring and predictable when we stay within the confines of what we are used to. People different than we are can offer beautiful ways to get out of that rut and get more out of life. They can help us solve problems if we maintain intellectual humility enough to understand that what we don't know is so much more than what we do. I firmly believe that the beginning of wisdom is the realization of how much we don't know...not how much we do.

That oddball bunch on TV known as "The A-Team" seemed to be a collection of social extremes. As individuals, each of them could easily be seen as strange enough in their own way to be considered outcasts. As a team, however, their range of capabilities was dramatic. Things that most of the team—or the rest of us, for that matter—considered impossible would be tackled one by one by a member of the team with a different perspective and approach to problems. For me, being on a real A-Team, I learned about some of the value of diversity when the need to hotwire a car arose. That wasn't something I knew how to do, or ever wanted to, but now it became something we absolutely needed. Thankfully, one of our guys knew how. He never answered why he was proficient at hotwiring cars. Maybe that's not the most illustrious example promoting diversity, but thank God for a wide range of talents and skills out there. It's our job to utilize them for good outcomes.

Once again, communication is paramount. Because we are all different and, as we are bringing different stuff to the table, we must establish a means to share the responsibility and credit. Skills and talents not brought to light, acknowledged, or understood can't possibly be put to work properly. No communication, no team.

In the planning process, you'll find that everyone has different ideas for how to get things done. That's okay. This doesn't mean that it's time to ignore everyone and jam your own ideas down their throats even if you are the boss. Now is the time to benefit from all the experience on your team. This is where diverse backgrounds can be a winning resource. But with everyone's head going in different directions, how do you manage a process to steer them all into a specific plan for success? It can feel like herding kitty cats. With the right process, though, all the best ideas can be combined to make a bombproof plan. Here's how.

Developing a Bombproof Plan

Divide the team into several planning groups (or cells), or individuals, depending on how many you have. A minimum of three, but no more than six, seems to work best. Each planning cell you have should be provided with a solid description of the task, conditions, and standards at hand. Knowing that each group will have entirely different ideas is part of the process. In fact, the more different these ideas are from one another, the better the process can be, until, ultimately, the plan is adopted.

Once the planning cells have decided on how they would accomplish the task at hand, then, one by one, they need to make an oral presentation of the plan and be prepared to answer questions from the rest of the team. A comparative analysis needs to take place as the plans are presented by the leader of each cell. Instead of going with subjective feelings about the details of the plans, though, a structure needs to be created that allows for more objective criteria in plan development. The merit of a given plan has to be based on more than opinion, as that can create division within the team and is often not the best basis for comparison.

First, consider the primary tasks involved with executing the plan like transportation, communication, and supply. Then list key desirable elements of execution, such as speed, stealth, and minimal expense. Once you've listed what needs to be done and what elements, qualities, or advantages are desirable, you can begin to evaluate and compare the merits of each plan. Assigning respective scores to the elements of each plan will numerically illustrate the strengths and weaknesses of each plan. While one plan will have the highest overall score (usually), it is often best to see if stronger elements from the other plans can be substituted or incorporated for an even better overall execution plan. This works to harness the best ideas for a combined plan in which the whole team participates.

Some take a passive approach during execution phase, simply observing what happens and how. I've heard too many times that "it's too late now" once things are underway. That may be true sometimes, but not always. Changing on the fly can be better. Leadership styles make a big difference, and this is where keeping your head pays off. I've known wonderful people, some of the best workers anywhere, who nevertheless were not good leaders. These hard workers are among the most productive people you could ever hope for, but they feel so compelled to immerse themselves in the labor of things that they lose sight over the greater objective at hand, thereby losing awareness and control.

To me, a leader can't be on the catwalk, keeping an eye on things, if he is down in a ditch with a shovel. It is entirely honorable to be a hands-on person, and it will pay off in many ways, but, in leadership, the truth is that a watchful eye over everything is necessary. In the military, we call it "command and control." When just enough distance is maintained, a leader can better observe the overall situation. This makes it possible to identify where change is needed. To be just detached enough allows a leader to remain mobile and glean information from key elements from the most advantageous position at any given time. It also allows communication to occur more effectively throughout.

The simple question "How's it going?" can put any member of the team in a critical role for success at any moment. As a junior enlisted member, I remember clearly how it affected me when a leader engaged with me and asked a question. There were typically two reactions I had when that happened: If I had been engaged and motivated, then I was eager to greet questions from the command; however, if I'd been half-stepping, and not as involved as I should have been, I would avoid questions at all cost.

Most of the time, I just didn't anticipate that leaders would have any interest in what I might say either way. When they asked me, though, it either kept my head in the game, or it got me there quickly. The idea that I might be a contributor of any significance made me happy. In fact, it made me shoot for the stars because I wanted to be a good soldier. This became an important lesson for me as a leader: to do unto others—you know the rest. Having an opportunity to represent yourself well and to be recognized means a lot. We should never forget that.

Communication during the execution phase improves outcomes. Either it allows immediate change that can contribute to improvement and success, or it can at least present food for thought in future applications. After all, communication is the product of the current experience, and only communication can allow it to be useful to the team.

After the Action Is Done

Once an event or activity has been conducted, there can be a lot of buzz over what went wrong. Impressions and feelings will vary among individuals after a group effort, and takeaways from the event can be hit-or-miss. Don't leave it up to individual impressions. As soon as possible after any event or activity, gather the team together to have a complete look at what transpired. The questions that need to be asked in open forum are:

- ▶ What was planned for?
- ▶ What actually happened?
- ▶ What went well?
- ▶ What didn't go as well as it could have?
- ▶ What are lessons learned?
- ▶ What are action items to improve next time?

With everyone involved and encouraged to speak, this after-action review can be a comprehensive basis for improvement. It is a mistake to force future teammates to re-invent the wheel because you didn't learn any lessons from an action. Each person gains traction as a significant contributor when they get the opportunity to influence future operations. Again, communication allows great things, but, without it, nothing seems to get better.

As a leader, make sure you are heard. More importantly, make sure you are listening.

No communication, no team.

8

HOW TO RULE THE BATTLEFIELD IN WAR AND LIFE

Preparation Is Key to Outmaneuvering the Enemy

"A true leader has the confidence to stand alone, the courage to make tough decisions, and the compassion to listen to the needs of others. He does not set out to be a leader, but becomes one by the equality of his actions and the integrity of his intent."

—GENERAL DOUGLAS MACARTHUR

Before starting out on a mission, an A-Team gets their gear in order and memorizes the maps and all the minute details of the mission and the contingency plans. Ruling the battlefield in war, business, and life requires smart preparation because there isn't often time to think when you're in the throes of battle. A football team that can easily shift to a proven strategy without a huddle when the clock is ticking off precious seconds is a winning team.

Another dilemma is what I call "the good idea fairy." My biggest problem with corporate culture is there often is no effective execution phase. The good idea fairy lands, but action items are not assigned, people aren't clear about what they are supposed to do, and so, six months later, someone brings up the idea again and everyone wonders what happened. The secret to execution is defining and assigning actionable goals to the right people. Intelligence Preparation of the Battlefield

(IPB) is also a key to commanding the operational environment you are in. Your team must be able to not only identify competitors and enemies to their success, but also know as much as possible about them—innocent as doves, sure, but wise as serpents too. Here are the secrets to how an A-Team prepares to rule the battlefield and then executes the mission.

I like to bring things down to basic concepts, when possible. I don't usually like lists, but when there's so much to keep up with, I need them. Staying in charge and in control requires a wide range of concerns that can quickly get out of control, or, at least, slip from awareness. A list of procedures that has been tested over time and under fire can really help to to keep the team on track. Rogers' Rangers, that famed mid-18th-century provincial company from the colony of New Hampshire, had "Standing Orders" that began with:"Don't forget nothing!" I don't know about you, but "not forgetting nothing" might be impossible for me. Written guidelines or a list saves the day for me. I need reference.

In the Army, it's important to get something going and to stay on top of it. Initiative and momentum are important factors, internally and externally. On the battlefield, getting the ball rolling and keeping it rolling is the way to seize initiative and win. Honestly, I don't see it as any different anywhere else in life, except that the stakes aren't usually as high. For me, there are certain things I miss about the military, but, for the most part, I can bring that kind of order, structure, and dependability with me in the way I continue to do things anywhere in life. One of the most effective things in the way I live my life and conduct business wasn't learned from the Special Forces at all. It came from my earliest leadership training in the regular Army. It's called "Troop Leading Procedures." Anytime your work involves a team of any kind, these TLPs can help. To me, they are equally useful whether I'm prepping for combat or getting the family ready to go on vacation. Let's see if I can translate them well enough to make them useful for applications in life that have nothing to do with the military. I want you to see Troop Leading Procedures the way I do, as an everyday asset. I'm telling you this is a system and a reference that can make you look great and smart, whether you are or not. Just take it from me.

First, we'll take a look at the military version of it. Here are the TLPs:

Troop Leading Procedures

Step 1: Receive the Mission

This may be in the form of a warning order (WARNORD), an operation order (OPORD), or a fragmentary order (FRAGO). Analyze it using the factors of Mission, Enemy, Terrain, Troops, Time available, and Civilian considerations (METT-TC).

1. Use no more than one-third of the available time for planning and issuing the operation order.
2. Determine what are the specified tasks (you were told to accomplish), the essential tasks (must accomplish to succeed), and the implied tasks (necessary but not spelled out).
3. Plan preparation activity backward from the time of execution.

Step 2: Issue a Warning Order

Provide initial instructions to your soldiers in a WARNORD. Include all available information and update as often as necessary. Certain information must be in the warning order:

1. The mission or nature of the operation.
2. Participants in the operation.
3. Time of the operation.
4. Time and place for issuance of the operation order.

Step 3: Make a Tentative Plan

Gather and consider key information for use in making a tentative plan. Update the information continuously and refine the plan as needed. Use this plan as the starting point for coordination, reconnaissance and movement instructions. Consider the factors of METT-TC:

1. **Mission.** Review the mission to ensure you fully understand all tasks.
2. **Enemy.** Consider the type, size, organization, tactics, and equipment of the enemy. Identify the greatest threat to the mission and its greatest vulnerability.

3. **Terrain.** Consider the effects of terrain and weather using observation, concealment, obstacles, key terrain and avenues of approach (OCOKA).
4. **Troops available.** Consider the strength of subordinate units, the characteristics of weapon systems and the capabilities of attached elements when assigning tasks to subordinate units.
5. **Time available.** Refine the allocation of time based on the tentative plan and any changes to the situation.
6. **Civilian considerations.** Consider the impact of the local population or other civilians on operations.

Step 4: Start Necessary Movement

Get the unit moving to where it needs to be as soon as possible.

Step 5: Reconnoiter

If time allows, make a personal reconnaissance to verify your terrain analysis, adjust the plan, confirm the usability of routes, and time any critical movements. Otherwise, make a map reconnaissance.

Step 6: Complete the Plan

Complete the plan based on the reconnaissance and any changes in the situation. Review the plan to ensure it meets the commander's intent and requirements of the mission.

Step 7: Issue the Complete Order

Platoon and smaller unit leaders normally issue oral operations orders.

1. To aid soldiers in understanding the concept for the mission, try to issue the order within sight of the objective or on the defensive terrain. When this is not possible, use a terrain model or sketch.
2. Ensure that your soldiers understand the mission, the commander's intent, the concept of the operation and their assigned tasks. You might require soldiers to repeat all or part of the order or demonstrate on the model or sketch their understanding of the operation.

Step 8: Supervise

Supervise combat preparation by conducting rehearsals and inspections.

1. **Rehearsals.** Use rehearsals to practice essential tasks, reveal weaknesses or problems in the plan, and improve soldier understanding of the concept of the operation.
   - Rehearsals should include subordinate leaders briefing their planned actions in sequence.
   - Conduct rehearsals on terrain that resembles the actual ground and in similar light conditions.
2. **Inspections.** Conduct pre-combat checks and inspections. Inspect:
   - Weapons, ammunition, uniforms and equipment.
   - Mission-essential equipment.
   - Soldiers' understanding of the mission and their specific responsibilities.
   - Communications.
   - Rations and water.
   - Camouflage.
   - Deficiencies noted during earlier inspections.

In planning and preparing for missions, you supervise the execution of tasks and insist on meeting the standard. You ensure your soldiers have what they need to do the job and (you?) make sure they take care of their equipment and themselves. This really means checking. You check your soldiers and subordinate leaders before, during, and after operations—not to "micro-manage" them, but to get an accurate status of your soldiers, and because their well-being is important to you. As my first squad leader, SGT Randolph, always said, "Don't expect unless you inspect."

Now let's take some of the military jargon and application out of it to see how TLPs might apply to us in anything we do. Instead of Troop Leading Procedures, let's just call them Leader Actions. As a leader, prepare your team for success in an activity using good leader actions. Leader actions are steps in a process that a leader uses to plan and conduct any activity from the time planning starts until the activity is completed. (The sequence of the leader actions is not always the same. They can be modified for the activity, the situation, and available time.)

Leader Actions

Receive a concept, and develop initial action items.

Repeat the instructions and conditions to the one who told you, ensuring that you understand correctly. Next, map out the sequences that must be done to accomplish the mission. Include "reverse planning," which simply means beginning your schedule with the end time and working back to the present. This ensures factoring the most key goals in the plan, rather than just beginning with now and trying to trace a timeline forward. Reverse planning keeps the goal in focus and prioritizes it, reducing time wasting on the front end.

What is the time schedule? Only one-third of the time available should go to the leader and chief planner. The bulk of the work in preparation lies with the team. The performance of the objectives will be done by the team, so the team gets priority. Time is often our most valuable resource, so as a leader, use no more than one-third of the time available for your preparations and make sure that the team gets at least two-thirds of it to go about the work of making success happen. Too often we dump a plan on our people at the last minute and don't give them enough time to do it well. This drives stress levels up and precipitates failure.

Tell or warn your team what's coming.

Alert your team of upcoming activity. It doesn't matter how you do it; just don't wait for all the information. Tell them now! Update the team when information becomes available. It may take several updates.

Come up with a rough idea of how to get it done.

This is the basis for your whole plan. This gives your team the information they need to complete a plan. Ask a lot of questions as you study the activity. What can get in the way? What's the location, environment, and weather? Who is involved?

What time is available for planning, activity, and transportation? Develop possible plans.

Analyze possible plans. Compare possible plans. Decide on one plan.

Begin preparations and assigning tasks.

Have your team where they will need to be early. Send team members with tasks to accomplish toward the team goal. As a leader, you may need to meet up with the team later. Choose one or more junior leaders to help the team follow your guidance and the overall plan, especially if you are not with them.

Gather as much information as possible.

Personal observations, brochures, maps, photographs, internet search… and so on. This is a continuous process during your leader actions, before, during, and after planned activity.

Complete a plan.

Make final decisions and communicate, communicate, communicate (with everyone involved). You might have to change the course of action if the situation is not what was expected. This is what really makes a leader! Make sure that your final plan still matches the original instructions!! Changes throughout planning can distract any leader from their higher leader's intent.

Share the plan with your team.

Do this is in writing and verbally. Ask questions to ensure understanding and compliance, and remain open to suggestions.

Supervise.

Inspect all involved equipment and those in attendance. The leader inspects everything or has subordinate leaders inspect. You may delegate your authority; you may not delegate responsibility. This is a continuous process. Rehearsal is very important for anything done as a group, as well as critical tasks for individuals. If it can be rehearsed within the time available, then it should be done! Have team members repeat their individual actions verbally to you. Try to access the real place for rehearsal, if possible. Always try to use the exact equipment you will be performing with during rehearsals.

It's easy to lose sight of a sequence. It's always easy to get distracted or to lose focus. References like this give us handrails, where we might otherwise have to rely solely on our talents. Resilience is a key trait to develop for ruling the battlefield in war and in life. A lack of resilience will certainly keep us from staying the course. Much like leadership, resilience can be seen as something we are born with, something that is learned, or both. I like to think that the product of our experience yields better resilience automatically, though I know that's not always true. Our posture and approach to life and work have everything to do with how we handle adversity. The inclination to maintain any sort of posture is generated by our mindset, and it is often influenced by spirituality, social status, gender role, ego, or any of a wide variety of motivators. What motivates one can be significant to them, yet petty to another. The real question is whether one's motivation is true enough to stand any meaningful test. When we stand to lose something or pay a high price, we tend to reevaluate what motivates us and what we believe in. When that gets shaken, folks can fall by the wayside, and you lose teammates.

Staying in the fight and staying on top takes tenacity and focus. Over time, things that test you can become cumulative challenges, or even burdens. Awareness of Post-Traumatic Stress and Critical Incident Stress have blossomed, to say the least. The mental aspects of traumatic exposure get a lot of attention now, and even produce financial benefits as a form of disability. In my opinion, this is evidence that we all need better ways of managing stress and preparing for some bad stuff that simply comes with living. This is especially true when we volunteer to place ourselves in harm's way.

Are we surprised when we witness death as a soldier or a cop? We shouldn't be. In professions that require us to run toward danger, not away, there has to be an acceptance of risk. Sure, we train to reduce that risk where possible, but by the time a threat has been identified, harm has already been done, in many cases. I feel that more needs to be done on the front end to prepare for these stressors. One is simply to surrender to the fact that we are human and that we fail. We should surrender to faith and love. We should surrender to the reality that we're really not that tough, and that we decline—all of us. Our decline can happen over decades, or it can even happen in a few short weeks. Sometimes our decline happens in an instant, and injuries take our capabilities away from us immediately. Whatever happens, we do not remain the way we picture ourselves in the prime of our lives.

So, with no question as to whether, but only *when*, we will lose elements of the self we rely on, resilience becomes the key to survival and winning. Our physical self does not stay as "bombproof" as we want it to. We endure things that test our emotions and our mindset. Having the right purpose and the right perspective go a long way toward maintaining focus in order to win in battle and in life.

The media has always enjoyed capturing the shock and dismay of soldiers taken by surprise by deployment. Of course, these individuals have accepted paychecks many times, and likely for years, before they were called to mobilize in any real way. In the military, peace is not the profession. Hopefully, peace will result from what is done, but no one should be shocked or even surprised to go through training, wear a uniform, draw a paycheck from the American taxpayer…and then be called to war. In this case, a moderate dose of reality is all that's required to keep folks from unraveling from the military experience. Somehow, people escape the truth and reality of what they have put themselves into. Bad call. This hurts the resilience of the team.

It is my humble opinion that those most affected in life after critical incidents are also the ones least prepared to face such experiences. This is certainly not an indictment against them, as there is no instruction manual for how to prepare for things that are horrible to live through. But the feeling of helplessness and vulnerability is what is most at issue, in my experience. I've always said that psychological issues are more likely to befall those less prepared to face present dangers. Those feelings of helplessness and vulnerability exist in most of us, but they get exaggerated by an inability to face them head on. I feel bad for military personnel who face the dangers of rocket attacks, suicide bombers, and IEDs, but never get the chance to fire back. I've gotten to face the enemy, fight him, and live to tell of it. I've even gotten to come home to my free country with honor and have been treated honorably. Our beloved Vietnam veterans were afforded no such luxury.

So, as something of a spoiled brat in our military history, I don't really have shadows creeping up on me. I feel thankful to have such purpose in life, and so much worth fighting for. As for getting wounded, joining the military was the right thing to do, even with the knowledge that so many had been hurt and killed before me. Why would it cease to be the right thing to do just because I'm the one who got hurt in this case? Injury is a part of it. I accept that. I thank God for the examples of men and women before me who served and sacrificed, reserving all they had left for continued service in any capacity possible for them. Thank you, General George Washington! Thank you all!

There are always others who have it worse, so it's important that we not isolate ourselves in misery, with nothing but complaints. Context helps. We are not the first to endure, to suffer, to fail. It is a human experience that requires enough humility to accept that it ain't all flowers. That doesn't mean it sucks, so stop looking for a perfect life. It doesn't exist. In the Special Forces, I often heard the phrase "embrace the suck!" I like that because it creates a better acceptance of lesser stuff. That's important if we are to aspire to being better people and better teammates. We have to be able to think of and support others while things aren't the best for ourselves. Great resilience comes in not dwelling on hardships or adversity, but making the best of everything. To count our blessings is key to a positive mindset. To recognize small victories is happiness. Stop screwing up the environment for others by whining about stuff that all of us face.

During my Special Forces Qualification Course at Fort Bragg, NC, I remember suffering an icy month in the field. I just couldn't believe it was that cold in the South. I've learned since that an ice storm or two is normal each year down there. At the time, it felt like this was the hardest and worst class ever in history, and that it was unfair, inhuman, and anything else I could think of to say to prove that I should be anywhere else. It was one of the many times in my career when I questioned whether they could really get away with doing this to us or not. This was always immediately followed by the reality that I had volunteered, and that I could quit at any moment with no adverse action.

The ice always melted on contact with our bodies, and was just enough to soak our gear and clothing. The wetness threatened to refreeze, and often did, stealing any warmth we struggled to generate. As we had absolutely no shelter and no escape for days and weeks, our perception of reality began to change. Suck became the norm. In one way, that's really hard. In another, I saw and felt things I never had before and this experience has actually improved my outlook on life. The best example I can use, though there are many, is about Bob.

My friend and fellow candidate, Casey, was often one of my battle buddies during that training. We usually wound up pulling security together, lying down in the icy terrain, which became wet under our bellies, and facing outward to guard against any approaching threat. In the priorities of work for a combat patrolling element, we had to take turns doing everything. Everything. Minimal movement is necessary on the perimeter of your occupied area, as it is closest to the potential enemy presence. For this reason, it was necessary to back up from the line a bit, if not to the center of the circle, for safe conduct of routine functions. Eating, sleeping, cleaning, defecating…it all had to be done within the circle of guys facing outward to maintain a 360-degree security perimeter at all times. Often, we would alternate short periods of sleep. Often, neither of us could. We were too miserable. Being cautious to avoid the attention of those unmerciful instructors, we would interact to keep from going out of our minds, though the right thing to do didn't include unnecessary interaction.

The coldest time always seemed to be at the onset of daylight. It's when you feel like the cold night might lose its grip on you. Instead, it felt colder for a time, and it became impossible to avoid shivering. Neither of us wanted the other to see us shivering, at first, but that went away with the realization that neither one of us could help it, anyway.

One morning, as daylight came, revealing the first clear sky in over a week of freezing temperatures, Casey got my attention with an excited whisper. "Hey, Stube! Bob's coming!"

I had absolutely no idea what he was talking about, and, for a moment, I questioned whether he was in his right mind.

"It's Bob, Stube!"

I lay there, freezing and shivering, half pissed off by his antics. I think I just wanted to be miserable. I didn't even feel like figuring out what the heck he was talking about, even though he was more animated now than I'd ever seen him. As he persisted with this "Bob" thing, I began to consider who that might be. Were we anticipating a visit from the commander? What was his first name, anyway? It wasn't uncommon for someone to lighten things up with an overly personal reference to a high-ranking individual by calling them by their first name, and I wondered if this was what he was doing.

Casey reached over and grabbed a hand full of my shirt and twisted it, shaking me back and forth with it.

"Damn, Casey," I said quietly. I was reluctant to go along with his antics for fear of drawing the attention of the wolves that were our teachers and assessors out there. I also didn't want to make myself vulnerable to being fooled, as I had pulled some fast ones on others. We all did to keep from being too serious all the time.

Then Casey just went limp, rolling backward onto the ground. He slowly raised his arms and hands toward the horizon. Now he was making short and fast grunting noises and breathing deeply with excitement like a caveman with no words. As he reached with arms, hands, and fingers extended, I saw it. Looking at where he was reaching toward, I saw the edge of the sun emerging. It was the same sun I'd seen and known my whole life, but this was different. In the most primitive way, Casey was showing great pleasure and excitement for the sun coming up this day. It was a big joke, but it was so serious. We were suffering, and this was the only thing available to help mitigate what I honestly describe as pain and anguish. He said, "It's Bob!"

"Bob?" I asked.

"Yeah," Casey responded. "Big…Orange…Ball."

A part of me wanted to act like it was stupid and childish. A bigger part of me felt wonderful about the prospect of B-O-B warming us up. You see, everything would be better in life at that time if we could just stop shivering and feel a little warmth. The sun's light and warmth are blessings that I'd taken for granted all of my life. Casey died during his service a few years after that, still a young man, but he gave me an incredible gift out there in the ice that will always make my life better. Bob will always have my awareness and appreciation. Casey will too.

Many experiences like the one with Casey in the field have helped teach me how to stay in the fight. They taught me that a certain element of unpleasantness or discomfort will usually accompany us throughout our earthly existence. The context that neither are we alone in these experiences, nor are we the first, actually helps. Only then can we accept that it is normal. My belief that we had it harder in that class than anyone ever did, and that we suffered more than anyone else had, was simply false. It was selfish to think that way. The failure to use proper context for life on Earth as a human is a barrier to success. Failure to identify blessings, assets, and other positives is to deny the resilience we need to keep our morale high and be good to one another.

When bad things happen, we swear never to take things for granted again. Yet we do. Keep up the fight for the mindfulness you'll need to rule the battlefield of life, business, or family.

9

THE SECRET TO A-TEAM EXECUTION

The Plan Is Everything Until it Isn't

"Leadership is the art of getting someone else to do something you want done because he wants to do it."

—DWIGHT D. EISENHOWER

While serving as cadre at the John F. Kennedy Special Warfare Center and School, I had a student named Riley Stephens. I didn't like him. Personally and professionally, I saw nothing of value in him. I simply judged him harshly and felt very negatively about him. To my great relief, Staff Sergeant Stephens failed to meet the standards in training. My recommendation was NTR, or Never to Return. I felt so strong in my dislike for him that I couldn't picture how he had made it as far in training as he did. I even felt as though my own Green Beret would have less value if he got one. He was stealing my oxygen, and the sound of his voice grated on my nerves.

Riley Stephens was gone! I was glad. I told him when he left that my own dad would be pissed if I passed someone who wouldn't be able to save my bacon in combat. Apparently, he did well after that because he received strong recommendations to make it back into the Special Forces' candidacy. It wouldn't have been my place to raise an objection to this as I had left my instructor position to rejoin a combat unit.

This Stephens guy went all the way back through all that tough training again. This time, he passed. I found out because he was on the A-Team I later joined for the big mission during which I was wounded.

The real wakeup call with Riley Stephens came when I was lying wounded on the battlefield surrounded by some guys who couldn't possibly save my life. They kept telling me to hang on, that the medic was on the way. Don't get me wrong. I had some great and heroic help, but not the kind that could actually save my life in that condition. I was dying. They said, "Here he is, Stube!" Then I saw the medic running up to my feet with that big aid bag. It was Riley Stephens.

My pain was horrible, like nothing I'd ever imagined. The traumatic damage and burns were unbearable. Yet, when I saw Riley, these words came quickly: "No hard feelings, right, Stephens?"

His eyes were wide with concern and professionalism as he performed a rapid trauma assessment on me. It was clear that he wanted so badly to save my life. It was also clear that he wanted to prove to me that he could do this now—when it counted. He could save my bacon. Riley hit all the marks of a flawless trauma medic. He stopped the hemorrhaging in multiple places. He dressed burns and so much more. He had become a better medic than I was, and, for the first time, I could feel pride in it. Before my own life was on the line, it would have been an insult to me that a student could be better than I. What an ego. Now I know that it is necessary that we give everything we have to the next generation. If they are not better than us, then we are failing. Yet another example of how I needed this to get the chip off my shoulder.

Though I should have been long unconscious by that time, I had the blessing and the curse of being fully aware of everything happening. As an SF Medic, I was very concerned with everything being done, and how. I remember feeling like I didn't need to worry anymore. I saw that he had firm command over my survivability. He and the good Lord had both had hands on me that day.

As I witnessed my teammates and commander clearly upset by my condition, I started feeling upset too. I was getting indicators that they thought I would surely die. Taking a page out of Chief Stube's playbook, I tried to get Riley's attention as my teammates carried me on the litter toward the medevac Blackhawk two hours after I'd been hit. I couldn't speak up loudly, so I reached up toward Riley, who was at my right shoulder at that moment. As I reached toward him and strained to speak his name over the noise of the battle and the helicopter there to take me out of the battlefield, he noticed my effort. Immediately, Riley screamed out to the crew with a true sense of urgency. "Put him down easy. Now!" As the litter touched the ground, there was a whole team of heads bending over me to see what was wrong, and everyone got silent. I used all the strength I had to speak up. "Riley, when I get…back…to Kandahar…I'm…telling everyone…you…touched…my…penis!"

I think it worked. I could see humor and relief in everyone. Riley seemed on the verge of tears, though, as he uttered words to the effect of, "Stube, you son of a bitch…."

I just couldn't stand the thought of everyone being down, even if I *was* going to die. The guys hoisted me up once more and marched me toward the noise and the rotor wash of my green chariot. To Kandahar I went, but, in my mind, it was to the unknown.

I saw Riley back at Fort Bragg a few months later, when I got a pass from the hospital to go home for a few days. When he stood before me, all I could do was cry. I was overwhelmed with gratitude and guilt. So grateful for how he had worked to save my life, and so guilty for the way I had judged him and cast him away. Also, I felt guilty that friends we shared had been killed, but I survived. Riley hated to see me broken like that, and he quickly wrote his name and number on a Post-it note to hand to me. He put his hand firmly on my shoulder and walked away. He was saving me from the embarrassment of crying, and it also seemed that he had had a hard time dealing with it.

I put the note on my computer monitor at home and made firm plans to be in touch with him. Riley Stephens had gone from being a man I despised to someone on my permanent Christmas card list. I now wanted my son to know him and be mentored by the hero who had saved my life. But what was different about Riley now? Or was it me? The answer is that Riley had always had it in him to be that professional, warrior, and hero. The sad truth is that I didn't have it in me to overcome perceived differences and focus on absolute commonalities. God put this one right in my lap. Why hadn't I mentored him when I caught negative indicators? Why had I kept him at arm's length, salivating for the opportunity to fail him? This had been my failure, not his, and that wouldn't be the last time I cried over it.

A couple years later, I still had not called him. I did not send a Christmas card. I had not taken my son to be around Riley Stephens. While I had been focused on myself, my recovery, and my new life after the military, Riley had been back in combat multiple times. I was still thinking of myself when the call came in that Riley had been killed in Afghanistan. The medic on scene could not save him. My considerations for building and maintaining a team changed in that moment. How could I have been, and stayed, so selfish?

I look back now and know that all of that highlights the secret to A-Team execution. There is a common bond that pulls an A-Team together. It is so strong that no one is irreplaceable. I was replaceable. Riley was there as junior medic. We'd foreseen and prepared for landmines and snipers. They knew how to get me out. The plan had been disrupted, but everyone shifted to take care of the problem as they were trained to do and then moved on with the plan. They were improvising, sure, but they weren't totally off script because they had prepared for worst-case scenarios.

An A-Team doesn't have a separate brain and a body. Every member can quickly and effectively communicate to alter the plan as needed. Special Forces are trained that way. Yes, there is a command structure, as there must be. But that doesn't mean that every part isn't also thinking and helping the plan evolve as communication goes up and down the chain of command.

This is how an A-Team moves forward as a cohesive unit—many different parts making the whole, and all of them working together for the same defined mission and with the same established values. I think this is why free peoples produce greater armies. We are used to thinking for ourselves. When we also learn to respect orders and our leadership, we become the best we can be. We become thinking parts of the whole. We share our ideas and what we see up and down the chain of command because we are all respected parts of the team. As professionals, we know what to share or to bother the team with and what to keep to ourselves. We know when to keep our mouths shut, but we also aren't afraid to speak up. That's a hard dichotomy for many to understand—and it might be impossible for someone from an authoritarian state to comprehend. America fosters inquisitive, creative minds; when these men and women also find the discipline to use their creativity and free spirits, they can be almost unstoppable. The key to team leadership and execution is fostering and funneling that leadership into a chosen direction, according to a plan. This is why, often, great leadership means getting out of the way.

This is the type of structure, of respect for each other and for leadership, that Green Beret A-Teams exemplify. I think this is also how successful sports and business teams function.

A Culture of Winning

Now we need a word on the human nature of the experience. Your team has been chosen, trained, has developed a plan and practiced the plan, and is now about to make it happen on the field of sport, business, or life.

As we move into the execution phase, excitement and anxiety can be heard in our voices and seen in our movements. The buzz of nervous energy fills the spaces between us, and our eyes grow a bit wider. These are realities even experienced Green Berets experience. It is the way that nervous energy is managed and dissipated that makes the difference. Training is what makes someone perform with confidence on the battlefield, on the playing field, or in the boardroom or sales meeting. As Ernest Hemingway wrote in *Men at War*: "Cowardice, as distinguished from panic, is almost always simply a lack of ability to suspend the functioning of the imagination." And this ability to suspend fear, or worries about losing an account or a game, come with training. We can create a winning culture by training and then executing according to plan and with team members who we know have our back.

I recall many nervous times in preparation when time was precious and scarce. There's nothing like a time crunch to ramp up anxiety. The professionals who mentored me showed me how to first steer into my own preparedness and have my stuff straight. If we want to avoid some of the anxiety, it's simple: Have your own stuff ready early!

Green Berets benefit from the experience and examples of the professionals around them. I cringe now because I know I was a turd who wasn't ready like others were. But that experience changed how I did things. It is clear to me now that being ready as an individual is crucial, not just for preparedness and team time management. Moreover (or, More than that), it is a great asset in dealing with the nervous feelings we all get to be able to focus on others and be helpful. If we are dealing only with ourselves and trying to keep up, then our anxiety will build.

When we increase our awareness of others, we minimize the kinds of mental strain that negatively impact performance. I remember times on combat patrols, both in training and in conflict, when it made a difference for me. I got to see it both ways. In times I was less prepared, I was struggling to get my stuff straight, even as the team began its movement. This added to my anxiety because my eyes and ears needed to have absolute focus on the movement at hand. Instead, I was worried and embarrassed that others would notice I wasn't ready, and I was frankly trying to unscrew myself instead of playing my expected role. Even if we get things squared away fairly quickly, it starts us off in a hurried and stressed way. Physical exertion may be a component of the mission, and now you're sweating and breathing hard prematurely. In the office, this is the person who shows up late and doesn't have their presentation or sales materials ready on time. You can feel the disrespect and tension from these people. They negatively impact a team. They wound you before you even begin.

Those who take their own preparedness seriously early are the better team players, and they are the ones who bail us out when we aren't ready as they are. They also leave themselves more awareness to apply to evolving situations and the needs of teammates. Those more individually ready will be the ones who catch problems and shortcomings early on and save the day. They see things we won't. The lesson is never to wait until the last minute to have your individual gear or material ready. Procrastinators hurt team progress and dynamics, causing a cascade of second and third order affects that challenge success at every turn. They will absorb and waste the goodness and diligence of others. Of all the resources to waste, we don't want it to be the talent our team has going for it. Get squared away early.

Another common trouble spot in the time of action is the surfacing of personal problems and breakdowns. This rarely happens in the Special Forces, but I see it all the time now. I'm not sure why, but people seem to wait for a critical event to demand attention for something that isn't right in their world. It's almost as if some folks just lose it when they don't get enough attention, and, worse, when the focus is on the greater team and a task at hand. I don't know if they feel their soul is getting lost or buried, but they seem to have a need to make themselves the most visible thing at important times, even if it means never being trusted or respected again.

It's true that we don't leave anyone behind as a cohesive team. It's also true that selfish and needy people who willingly distract team efforts in an execution phase may not be welcome on the next mission. I'm not talking about children's activities here. If an adult presents in this way, however, then extricate them from the team effort. Real issues, emergencies, and tragedies happen enough, and they deserve our best. This other stuff, however, is a distraction and a key indicator that someone might not be the team player you need.

Another question is whether your priority is to have friends and to support them if this friendship gets in the way of the team's success. It may sound hard, but the train wreck of a personal life needs to be prevented from pulling the mission down with it. The team you create will determine if it becomes a soap opera. This is where it really matters, because in the execution phase, you need to move without distractions.

Also, in the execution phase, you've gotta know your role. One of the biggest issues with this, as part of a team dynamic, is understanding how much latitude you have to make your own assessments and decisions. Most times, as members of a team, we just don't have enough information to make informed decisions independently. Even if we are the resident guru in some regard, we must still defer to those in charge, in the know, or who are simply in a better position at the moment. Never forget that nobody likes a ball hog. Pass the ball! This goes into issues of loyalty and humility in the name of the team and progress. Many can't see that their push to do so much themselves is selfish and inappropriate when it's out of their lane to do what they are doing. Whether physical or cerebral, crossing into the lane of others goes against good teamwork and can be a setback in overall execution. By all means, be all you can be and do all you can do. But know your role and stay in your lane. Wise people know it doesn't pay to support an appearance that you're in charge when you aren't. And don't seek attention for every little thing you do. That just proves you're doing it for your own image, not for the good of the team and the objective. In the end, our ability to work hard and take pride as contributors will be the truest indicator of our worth.

Refer to the Plan

When we've got the talking part done, and the good idea fairy has left the building, keep the Operations Order in mind. An Operations Order can save the day and get us on the way to winning.

Everything presented so far in this book can be applied in the following execution plan we call an Operations Order. The secret to A-Team execution is really not a secret at all. We just have to believe in the greater mission, believe in each other, and, moving forward, have a solid plan that everyone on the team is committed to. The following is a guideline for that kind of performance in implementing a plan for the success we want or need.

An Operations Order (OPORD) is simply a plan format meant to assist subordinate units with the conduct of military operations. An OPORD describes the situation the unit faces, the mission of the unit, and what supporting activities the unit will conduct in order to achieve their commander's desired end state. This basic format was developed by Frederick Edwin Garman while he was assigned to Fort Benning's Infantry School, Ranger & Tactics Department in 1957 to 1958. The Army quickly adapted it for standardized practice and required its use during the Vietnam War.

1. **SITUATION**
    a. Area of Interest
    b. Area of Operations
        - Terrain
        - Weather
    c. Enemy Forces
        - Composition, Disposition, and Strength
        - Recent Activities

- Locations and Capabilities
- Enemy COAs (Courses of Action)

d. Friendly Forces
- Higher HQ Mission and Intent
- Mission of Adjacent Units

e. Attachments and Detachments

2. **MISSION**

A concise statement that includes the Who, What, Where, When, and Why of the operation to be conducted.

3. **EXECUTION**

a. Commander's Intent

b. Concept of operations
- Maneuver
- Fires
- Reconnaissance and Surveillance
- Intelligence
- Engineer
- Air Defense
- Information Operations

c. Scheme of Movement and Maneuver

d. Scheme of Fires

e. Casualty Evacuation

f. Tasks to Subordinate Units

g. Tasks to Combat Support
- Intelligence
- Engineer
- Fire Support
- Air Defense
- Signal
- CBRNE (Chemical, Biological, Radiological, Nuclear, and Explosive weapons)
- Provost Marshal
- MISO (Military Information Support Operations, formerly Psychological Operations or PSYOP)

- Civil Military

h. Coordinating Instructions
- Time or condition when the plan or order becomes effective
- CCIR (Commander's Critical Information Requirements)
- EEFI (Essential Elements of Friendly Information)
- Risk Reduction Control Measures
- Rules of Engagement
- Environmental Considerations
- Force Protection

4. SUSTAINMENT

a. Logistics
- Sustainment Overlay
- Maintenance
- Transportation
- Supply
- Field Services

b. Personnel Services Support
- Method of marking and handling EPWs
- Religious Services

c. Army Health System Support
- Medical Command and Control
- Medical Treatment
- Medical Evacuation
- Preventive Medicine

5. COMMAND AND CONTROL

a. Command
- Location of Commander
- Succession of Command

b. Control
- Command Posts
- Reports

c. Signal
- SOI index in effect
- Methods of communication by priority

- Pyrotechnics and Signals
- Code Words
- Challenge and Password
- Number Combination
- Running Password
- Recognition Signals

That's a lot of military jargon, but it forces you to remember the details. By the time you go into the execution phase to complete a mission, a game, a business deal, and more, these details should be part of you. As the leader, if you are forced to change a facet of the plan, this change won't erase the plan. Everyone will know you simply tweaked the plan. If you are part of the team and think for some reason that the plan needs to be altered to deal with new or unforeseen circumstances, then you should pass that information up the chain. If you're on a good team, they will listen and respond accordingly.

Maintaining this kind of holistic perspective is the challenge, particularly when you're in the hot seat, but it is key to staying supple and fast enough to take advantage of opportunities and to avoid pitfalls.

Of course, if team members lose discipline, a plethora of uninvolved parties can interject at will about what you're screwing up or should do differently. Armchair quarterbacks and backseat drivers abound. It's telling how they choose to hide in the crowd and remain unidentified when we need a leader. They are nothing but that smartass in the back of the classroom who knows he's failing and tries to bring down the whole team instead of upping his game. In places and on teams where there is a leadership vacuum, they can do a lot of harm. In the absence of responsibility or accountability, they can destroy any hope of success.

Like so many other things I've pointed out, I don't believe this is solely beneficial to the military. If it works when folks have to overcome their fear of dying to get it done, isn't it of sufficient merit to be dependable in other less dangerous endeavors? If it is good enough to keep things moving in the right direction with warfare underway, wouldn't it be awfully good otherwise? It's more human than military, actually. The military stuff just ups the ante and attempts to take out some of the human error that prevails when the stress monkey gets on our backs.

So where does the magic in some leaders and teams come from? Is it a charismatic speech given at halftime that fosters such greatness? Is it overcoming tragedy and loss together that causes a team to unify and overcome? With every great victory, there seems to have been some kind of adversity involved that makes it all the more dramatic. The real answer people want is whether it's something they can create in their own lives or not. What we know for sure is that we love the feeling we get from even seeing it or hearing about it. Even more, being a part of it. This is part of what makes sports and war movies so popular. We want to see the team come together and to win.

My experience tells me that it isn't just the magic of the leading role that creates a winning environment and team. It isn't a story of adversity that turns it into a win. It is true that a good leader is likely to inspire people, but it's not true that a leader can turn everyone into a winner. It's true that adversity and tragedy can create an emotional charge, but that's not enough, either. In fact, in the intensity and fog of emotion, it's common for folks to break the rules, to go outside the lines or beyond normal limits. This seldom yields what you want it to, even though it looks good on the silver screen. I remember several times going out on a mission that we would personally and internally dedicate to a fallen buddy or unit member. It wasn't pretty how some vented their grief. Nothing bad happened, thankfully, but that kind of emotion can foster some faulty thinking and overly dramatic behavior that deviates both from the plan and the fundamentals of the game. Discretion is said to be the better part of valor, but if your buddy just got killed, the odds are high that you will use less discretion and wind up in a worse situation than you might in the absence of that emotion.

You can construct a team from people of great talent and capability, but will they be inclined to show enough positive attitude and effort to meet their own potential? You can select folks who put out all the effort in the world, and with a great attitude too, but if they lack the talent and capability to begin with, you just may not get there. It is surely a balance. When you pick your A-Team, you need to pick those with the requisite talent and capability, but also the mindset to generate attitude and effort, which are the only two vehicles to help bridge the gap to what we call potential. Without attitude and effort, potential would be quite an elusive thing.

A selection process with real standards becomes the single most important key to building the A-Team. It's hard to turn a turd into an ice sculpture, right? You know what they say. You can put a pig in a tuxedo, but it's still a pig. So A-Team execution will require the right team, first from the perspective of composition, which requires talent, capability, and character, and, second, considering the application of those things along the lines of attitude and effort.

A leader provides a special form of navigation and allows for better focus and application in the pursuit of potential. Their ability to do so will typically be no more effective than their intuitive ability or desire to see what potential they are working with. They have to know their people. They have to care.

All of this is beautiful and warm stuff, but getting something done has to become a thing of action. The good idea fairy needs to exit stage left so the execution phase can begin. If you're a team player, you'll be chomping at the bit to get started on things you know need doing or can be done.

Still, even at the execution phase, any room full of capable people will present huge leadership challenges. Everyone has the right answer or a better solution. Just ask them, and they'll tell you. This is the aforementioned difficulty of herding kitty cats, because if you don't achieve unity in purpose and method, then everyone will be doing their own thing—usually in different directions.

The planning and decision-making tools from previous chapters will all help to rein this in so you can now begin executing the greater plan. The great news is that with a method and a structure like the Operations Order provides, you don't even have to be a great leader to get it done well. You don't have to be a great communicator or an amazing inspiration to anyone. You just implement the execution plan by putting great people to work. It will always help to provide and enhance purpose, direction, and motivation.

The secret to A-Team execution is so very simple. That might sound cliché, but it's true. A more detailed version of the answer can be constructed through the chapters of this book, but I submit that it's just about the selection process to begin with, followed by a solid plan to follow and refer to throughout the given duration. Beyond that, there is a lot to work on and improve, but good people and a good plan are what make winning possible.

10

HOW TO STAY SUCCESSFUL AFTER WINNING

After the Euphoria of Winning, Teams Often Lose Focus

"Lead me, follow me, or get the hell out of my way."

—GEORGE S. PATTON JR.

You have now achieved your goal. Your family, business, or unit has successfully done what you have defined. You've completed the mission, and there's always some level of victory in that. Great! But, now, it's time to start over with a new objective along the same values. If you don't, you risk complacency and lack of focus that will make your team fall apart. Championship teams face this at the end of a winning season. Apple faces it now. An A-Team of Green Berets faces it after every mission. They stay engaged and cohesive because of the methodology outlined here. The most successful winners go right back to work immediately after a win. They choose to stay engaged with the kind of effort that brought them success. If they allow their own perception of themselves to change due to winning, then they will overlook or take for granted the kinds of requirements that ensured victory for them. It's very easy to be consumed by thoughts of victory and success. We tend to revel in it. If we lose, we focus on the preparation it will take to be better next time. If we win, we focus on the great performance and the status of being a winner. This particular recipe for failure has been the downfall of too many to count. Many times, it presents a major fall from grace in the public eye. When I observe athletes crying and sobbing over a defeat, I often wonder how their attitude might be different, or even their preparation and execution, if the stakes were higher. What if winning or losing meant life or death? Once again, I believe this is where we could all take a page out of the warfighter's playbook in order to better prepare for winning, and, especially, not losing.

Sound practices for winning should be observed if success is important to you and your team. Practical answers and common sense have to prevail. But much of the diligence a team routinely employs can suffer in the lax haze of celebration. It's not wrong to celebrate, but how long should we celebrate? I'm not talking about the party we have after the big win. I'm talking about the celebratory state of mind that can leave us in a posture that threatens future success. "I got mine!" Whether it's a Super Bowl ring or a master's degree, those three words are the enemy. No matter how great we once were, we turn ourselves into one of those self-propelled sandbags when we continue to bask in the glory of past accomplishments. We want to enjoy the advantages of such accomplishments, but it's important that we maintain the effort levels and the attitude expected of any such performer.

What we do each day should be aligned with the characteristics required to be that winner we brag about having been. In our own minds, and in the minds of certain others, we may have the good fortune of maintaining the image of that winner forever. But to those who count on us today, a win in the past doesn't satisfy current deliverables. Action items matter, and we all need to get to work. You will find yourself earning more respect if people see you as a hard-working and dedicated team player first and then just happen to find out about your great accomplishments.

So it comes back to humility again. For me, humility seems to be the single biggest factor in maintaining a winning attitude that works. The selfish interests we feel need to be mitigated by selfless behavior. That will ensure that we put the good of the team ahead of our own even when we don't feel like it.

I attended a wedding that had an effect on me in a couple of different ways. Primarily, I was affected by what the priest had to say there.

Maybe I've heard many of the same things before, but, somehow, my posture or disposition at the time allowed me to gather incredible power from what he had said. When talking about the marriage we were all about to witness becoming official, this priest dove into concepts that I felt should speak to everyone in the room, not just the young couple getting started on a life journey together. I knew it applied to me. He spoke about what it means to love someone and pledge your love to them. The way he addressed it made it relevant not just in marriage, but in life. Commitments are important. What I heard from him was big and wide in scope. The decisions we make to love or to serve need to be honored by us. Once we make that choice, it shouldn't even be approached as an option. This man said that the commitment we make to love someone has to remain in motion constantly as an action word. "Do it!" Once the commitment is made, it can no longer be something we do "because we feel like it." Rather, it is to become something we do whether we feel like it or not. That's big. For me, this describes the nature of service. To humble ourselves is necessary for our service to be effective. An attitude of gratitude is in order, as it is much easier to be humble when we count our blessings and keep an eye on the things that are worth serving to us and that we are grateful for.

A win is like anything else with people in that the definition of what constitutes "a win" is different for each person. It is certainly not always the trophy or your name at the top of a list. It's more personal than that. When I hosted a television show my first couple years out of the military, I named it *Coming Home with Greg Stube*. I absolutely did not want my name in the title, but, in an ironic twist, to call it simply *Coming Home* was not an option. This is because one of Jane Fonda's feature films had been named such. I was advised to personalize it and make it my own by adding my name to it. Anyway, my favorite part of that show was talking to people from all walks of life about what coming home meant to them. Each episode, I would get brief comments from locals everywhere. I would ask them in the most comprehensive way I could what they loved about coming home since childhood. It invoked the most personal things in life for most. What really grabbed my attention about it was the way I could see the wheels in their minds turning at first in order to define what "home" was to them. Each person viewed that simple thing in dramatically different ways. To some, home was a state or a town. To others, it was a farm or a house. An alma mater even held the special title of home for some. But I saw clearly what I was on to when a retired army general in Alaska said that home to him was no bigger than what he could put his arms around, and he named his wife. Beautiful.

So the way we define all things takes a personal spin, no matter how conventional words and their meanings might seem. Home is very personal, and so is a win. Whatever winning is to you will affect how you focus, what you do, and how you do it. It goes to core motivation and heavily influences resilience and the ability to stay the course in any endeavor. What things mean to you will certainly determine whether you will love them even when you don't feel like it. What a win is to you will also influence your threshold in what you're willing to do for or tolerate in a given pursuit.

Whatever meaning these things take on in our lives, both individually and as a team, we must find the collective purpose and value in our pursuits. I'm suggesting that, in the case of winning, the definition each person has for it can determine whether they are choosing a lifestyle and a standard in their life and work, or simply a short-term goal. If it is the latter, then the concern becomes whether they will continue to try, or even care, after a certain metric or achievement has been met.

The worst thing we can do is assume we're all in it for the big win. To my dismay, I learned that even in top-tier work, we are not. If we intend to stay successful as a team, then we must harness a collective goal and mindset that takes us past immediate victories. If we don't, we're likely to lose key individuals.

In my mind, winning is not an endpoint, but a symptom of good teamwork. Each win should enhance our humility and gratitude for all who make it possible. It should make us strive to be as useful to our teammates as they are to us. The right mindset is to know it will never be possible, and that we must remain in the hardworking posture that gratitude demands.

I had the good fortune of meeting President George W. Bush after I was wounded. He had just left office after his second term as President. When I met him, he gave me good food for thought on what a win really is. For just about anyone, becoming the President of the United States could be seen as the greatest win possible. To win that election and to be in that position is at the top of the heap, right? Apparently, not for W. His humility was so palpable to me that I could clearly see an absence of ego. What I saw and felt was center mass for the servant/ leader ethos. What he said confirmed it.

When I got to shake President Bush's hand, I concealed a Special Forces challenge coin in my hand for a smooth delivery, as most do. I had been introduced as an army guy who'd been severely wounded. The introduction alone had created a posture in the President that all could see and feel. He was so very respectful and responsive that you could see the personal responsibility he felt for (me, us?) being at war, and for the consequences that I had experienced. My strongest wish was for him to know that I was on board for the big win and had no reservations about it. I knew that military service always involved death and trauma, and I had signed up anyway. What kind of hypocrite would it make me to change my feelings on the validity of that service just because it was me who had gotten hurt this time? I wanted him to know that I believed he was right, and that I was one who continued to be proud to be on the team. On his team. On America's team.

In that brief moment of contact with him, there was no way to convey how I felt in any complete way. But what happened when he saw the coin is something that continues to validate me and compel me to be a team player and a servant/leader. The President looked at the coin I'd slipped into his hand with the handshake. He said, "You didn't tell me you were one of these guys!" He reached one hand behind my neck and upwardly slapped the back of my head like a good grandpa would do to his grandson. He welled up a bit, and, with absolute sincerity, said, "You know, I don't miss being the President for one minute. What I miss is being on the team with you guys."

I will never forget that, and it continues to inspire me. If being on the team and facing victory, hardship, and loss together is the win, then how could we ever lose? The humility and purpose in his comment embodies much of what it takes to stay successful after winning. Doing the right thing, doing it for the right reasons, and doing it well, is winning. To me, not even a Super Bowl victory fully defines a winning team, because so many honorable pursuits never produce a trophy or even an honorable mention. It's surely a subject to be pondered that the best warriors I've ever known and witnessed in action don't give a damn about awards or honors. They know that the most amazing acts will likely remain anonymous forever, and that high awards are often assigned for lesser things in the name of even lesser things still. They do what they do because they are on the team, and because it's the right thing to do. This can take many forms in our American lives too.

Life tends to change constantly, and everything seems to cycle through seasons. Winning feels like a season of its own. It is important to be mindful that as things rise to the peak of any great success, they must almost necessarily fall after it too. This is a part of things that most of us would rather not deal with. Euphoria fools us into thinking there is nothing to worry about on the other side of a great time. That's a threat. Whether these changes come quickly or far apart, continuing to succeed after a win will likely be a challenge we don't anticipate. It will take us back to work, stealing some of the glory of the win. It will put us back into the drudgery of daily routines, making us feel like we're not special, after all. It takes time to realize that the true identity and worthwhile endeavor we are after is only punctuated by wins. Winning is not a constant and cannot be assumed as the whole of our identity. The effort associated with winning can become an identity, and I have found it equally respectable whether that kind of effort actually results in a win or not. It is an honorable pursuit to do your best, and demonstrated commitments make us more valuable and trustworthy. Not everyone is a winner, but, to a degree, those who put such commitment and hard work into their pursuits are winners in life. A win is a temporary outcome. What it took to win is where reality lies, so get back into the work of it. Anything else is a form of complacency that victory tries to induce. I've heard it a million times not to make a sprint of it, but a marathon. I often visualize the life and times of General George Washington for perspective.

When we win, others can tend to view us as ninjas of some kind. Heck, it's easy to fall for the hype sometimes and to believe it ourselves. Thinking that we are above or beyond the basic mechanics of things is the worst thing we could do, no matter how "advanced" we get. Many fail to see that the best in any given field became that way through extensive rehearsal of the basics and application of fundamentals in a way that becomes repeatable to very high standards. It's not the fundamentals that change. It's the standards that do. It's not about ninjas. It's about hard work and dedication to fundamentals. The more seasoned we get, the more we feel like we are somehow "above" the most basic stuff we did as beginners. In everything I do now, I can see that it's a trap to feel that way.

I remember feeling insulted when I'd made it to the A-Team in the Special Forces but was still forced to rehearse basic stuff for hours and days at a time. Safety is a big reason I should have never felt that way, but there's so much more to it. Looking back, I can point to leaders who had maintained solid focus on proficiency, versus those who took it for granted and preferred super high morale, self-image, and overconfidence. It seems so simple and obvious now, but, at the time, I actually resented leaders who forced me to spend the time and effort it took to make me great at things that saved my own life. It's such a dangerous thing when we choose a great self-image over the hard work it takes to be solid. To have done well is no guarantee of doing well.

In Bosnia and Kosovo, our teams have faced varying threat levels over the years. It was very fresh and new when I came on board. Much of the new urban combat doctrine had been forced by events in the Balkans, and the fact was that combat training in the U.S. Military for decades had followed the Vietnam experience. The woods, jungles, and deserts dominated our training. Overcoming natural terrain is what we'd become proficient at. The problem was that the overwhelming majority of hostile action around the world and throughout history occur in urban environments. You know, where the people are. In this focal shift in our training, things got heavy in terms of shooting in and around buildings.

My first mission in Bosnia was preceded by more advanced and diverse training than I had ever been through in the military. By this time, I thought I was Rambo. With so much shooting under my belt, I felt like I was clearly above average. I didn't think I needed any more time on the basics. But when we got settled into our team house in the middle of a war-torn country, one of the first things my team sergeant had us do was a dry fire rehearsal with our primary weapons for that mission. Without a way to do live fire training locally, our team daddy made us line up facing a wall, wearing the same weapons set up the same way. Over the course of days, weeks, and months, we rehearsed the basics of drawing and firing our weapons in that configuration. Hundreds and hundreds of times, over and over, we would pick a spot on the wall in front of us and draw to fire with no ammo. When I started with it, I felt silly, and the boss saw that I wasn't excited about doing it. He said, "Okay, Greg! If this isn't enough action for you, then you just need to yell '*Bang!*' every time you draw." Then he made me do it. I was humiliated and embarrassed, particularly later, when my more experienced teammates expressed disappointment in me. I found out it was time to stop admiring myself and start going about the business of being a professional. It didn't take long before I could see my level of readiness improving. The more I did it, the better and faster and more accurate I got.

I'm very proud to live in a country that has a conscience. One of the responsibilities inherent to that commitment is being good at rapid discriminatory shooting, or not killing innocents. It takes practice to go into a room you've never seen before, where you anticipate bad guys with weapons already pointed at the door you're coming in, and not make any mistakes. I still feel angry with armchair quarterbacks who play God with these scenarios after the fact. Media, lawyers, and experts everywhere love to talk about what should have or shouldn't have happened sometimes. Yes, sometimes it does seem obvious, but, more often, you had to be there to figure it out. If you can't feel the fear and perceive the threat to your own life, then you have no metric on the situation. Many who criticize unfortunate events in war have never felt that kind of fear. In our free country, it's safe to say they've chosen not to. Yet the criticism pours in from those who don't know. I'm not suggesting that military actions go unchecked, but war is hell, not some academic vacuum of scenario-based training. If your buddy just got killed here, and you are following up to clear the area of the same bad guys that killed him, will you be unaffected or emotionally detached? I'm not sure it's possible to train all the human stuff out of us. In these situations, what is critical is that we are well rehearsed and can respond instantly and accurately in dynamic and fast-moving threat environments. Even without the emotions attached or the lives at risk, most cannot quickly and accurately discriminate with the use of deadly force between a fighting-age male with an AK-47 and a grandpa with a ukulele. It's a lot to put on a person. It challenges much of what we hold sacred or are comfortable with. It tests elements of cultural and religious rights and wrongs. Still, there's only one way to overcome all that and win. That's to practice so much that you can overcome parts of your humanity and minimize mistakes.

For me, this clarifies how lessons learned from the battlefield can help us continue to succeed after winning in any walk of life. Life in the Special Forces seemed to be one thing after another that could get you killed. The victory in it becomes a longer stretch and a way of life, as opposed to just winning a battle and coming home. In that line of work, you probably won't even be going home. Instead, you'll face more and more deadly events. It feels like the odds get stacked against even surviving to go home when you repeatedly cheat death and avoid explosions and bullets routinely. There's never a point where you can feel like you achieved a victory when you know the next random shot can kill you. There's also never a true personal victory to be had when you lose a teammate. After that, survival is just a guilt complex for life.

The very serious take away for me is that if folks like the SEALS and Green Berets can use these principles to maintain success in those environments, how much good can the same ideas and practices help life in all areas? It doesn't require high stress, risk, and threat to be that professionally driven and dedicated. We can work toward anything we want with successful posture and interdependence with the trustworthy people we know and love. Build your own A-Team at home, at work, or just for fun. Maybe with the example of warfare in mind, the answer is that we just can't allow ourselves the luxury of resting on our laurels. Getting lazy and complacent about what is ahead is bad, no matter what you've already accomplished. Imagine your weekend softball team with all that going for it!

But it's not just good intentions and positive mentality that get us where we want to go. Everyone knows the road to hell is paved with that stuff. Ongoing success after winning will take some homework. The previously mentioned "After Action Review" is a fantastic method for capturing or identifying elements of great planning and performance that work or don't work. Things captured immediately after an event will allow you to incorporate these things into future plans. This makes the AAR an important part of staying successful after winning. We all forget things, and we don't want that to happen with things that allowed for us to win. We also don't want to keep doing things that are a threat to winning, big or small. As discussed, including the entire extended team in an AAR will allow for better visibility on details from top to bottom, and it will allow for dynamic improvement for the future.

The tendency following a win is to feel as though everything obviously went well. We won! Well, it may have gone well enough to pull off the win, but that doesn't account for the external factors that could have cost us. The same can be true in day-to-day operations and life. We often don't know something is going wrong until we get externally observed or evaluated. We don't always know when we have debris dangling from our nostril. Someone else has to tell us, and, in that case, we hope it's a friend. Otherwise, we may experience failure on some level before we recognize there's a problem, much less diagnose what the problem is. A thorough AAR can help us identify both positives and negatives, and it can help us respond accordingly to enhance success.

An AAR is used following a specific activity or event. Because those occasions may be few or far between, they may not be comprehensive enough to catch potential trouble or inefficiencies. This is why a "hot wash" might be in order as a frequent practice. To me, a hot wash is an opportunity for the whole team to be in the same place together for a short time so they can, one by one, give a quick review on what they've done since the last hot wash, and what they intend to do next. I love this kind of compass check because it allows for clear direction, and for the left hand to know what the right hand is doing.

Teams build great interdependence, confidence, and much more when frequent communication and transparency are used liberally. Going around the room to hear what each person is doing ensures that they actually know what they are doing, and it allows for great management of individual and collective tasks going forward. It also cuts down on redundancy, allowing for immediate changes and corrections. You'll also find peer-driven solutions taking shape when teammates realize how they might help each other. Once again, your A-Team will want to be fully engaged and proactive. Frequent hot washes help everyone to stay on the cutting edge of things. They also foster verbal communication on the part of every individual, which helps all around, but, specifically, makes AAR time more productive and complete.

Famous coaches and military teams do not have a monopoly on great team building and leadership. Not even the ones in the movies we love to watch. It's not a military thing. It's not a sports thing. It's simply a human thing. It's good that we don't have to reinvent the wheel on this stuff, but it can be tough to gain clear examples and decipher or translate how to make it happen in our own little world. For me, it all gets easier when I decide to be strong enough and selfless enough to serve above self, and to be willing to serve beyond sacrifice.

Quitting is often a shameful thing, or, at least, it should be. The times in my life when I remember not following through were always marked by selfish interests and motivations that were near-sighted, immature, and not well thought out. I've seen a whole lot of it in high performance arenas, where you find out what you're made of when the cost or the sacrifice becomes apparent.

Do what you believe in. Try to stick to that. Don't fail others by not knowing yourself well enough when you make a commitment. It's true that we learn, grow, and change, so the balance becomes a matter of what we've figured out in terms of basic rights and wrongs. We may evolve in our ideas regarding advanced topics for as long as we live, but fundamentals come early and often never change. With a little intellectual humility, we can navigate on through our challenges without a major crash. But if we lack the ability to follow through, we've likely failed to have real values. Only we can fix this. Our success in any area is contingent on whether we want to be there in the first place. This can hardly work for something you're on the fence about believing in or are harboring resentment or cynicism for.

After all is said and done, and best practices aside, it is our core motivations, attitudes, and effort that set us apart in good or bad ways. Acting with selfish motivation fails teammates and peers immediately.

It will fail us even more as individuals, in the long run, taking the shape of remorse, regret, and shame. This is part of why it's paramount to believe in and serve for something that is greater than yourself.

In a book about building your own A-Team, one might not expect so much about self. From where I stand today, I can see some of the things my dad tried to advise me of more clearly than ever. If I want a better team, I need to look at the part of it I have the most control over—myself, myself, myself. When you adopt the best performance and values for yourself, it tends to change even your social life. Dad used to say, "Show me your friends, and I'll show you your future." I've lived long enough to see truth and wisdom in that. Winners gravitate toward other winners. Building your team will depend heavily on what you offer yourself as a teammate, and, in turn, the kinds of people you attract, to begin with. So I guess it is all about ourselves, but not in the immature ways we may have once thought.

In closing, I guess I want everyone to have the great fortune that I did, as I was part of something that pushed me to be better than I thought I could be. I want everyone to have the solid feeling that comes from being a solid part of a winning team. I want everyone to be able to cheat death, but at the same time to lose just enough to put proper value in what we too often take for granted.

I want us all to be able, even on bad days, to recognize that our absolute commonalities far outweigh our perceived differences. Don't wait for the tragedy to occur. Let's hug each other today and realize that we *do* need one another.

My wish is that we all learn to do as that priest said we ought to. We need to live up to the obligation of loving others, especially when we don't feel like it. Be kind. Put ourselves last. It seems like the worst place to be, but it feels better than anything.

I want men to embrace the feminine virtues that have made their lives whole and which have been the centerpiece of our culture and Fort Living Room for ages. The acceptance of love and compassion as leading characteristics in life is the only way to know true strength. Nothing else will endure or sustain us. Never forget the maternal nature that has given so many a safe place in the world, and comfort found nowhere else.

My hope for veterans is that we will all remain grateful for a country worth serving and defending, and that the purpose we gain in our lives through that service is immeasurably valuable. We should never cease to live with the kind of honor that made us raise our right hand and swear the oath in the first place. Banish sympathy, for we are not victims. Refuse to live wounded and choose to remain warriors, instead. Continue to serve, and to live forever in the words spoken by John F. Kennedy, "Ask not what your country can do for you, but what you can do for your country."

American veterans must stand to the end, giving what they can with whatever they have left, like so many did alongside George Washington. The entitlement class had better not ever include the American veteran. Pay forward the lessons learned in national service and on the battlefield, that the next generation may have a head start at being better than our own. We are failures if they are not. Oh, yeah, and if you are one of those fools who has just signed up for the college money, then, well, welcome to the big show. You'll be fun to watch.

My hope for civilians—those who serve in other ways—is that while so many have felt compelled on some level to serve, but did not do so in the military, it means nothing less of you. In fact, if you are an American in the homeland, doing your best, then you are part of the fabric of our country. If not for your contribution to the American way, it would be less than it is. Americans living their dreams and being their best is what makes this beautiful model of freedom worth fighting for. You are great, and our culture is strong. Because we have the freedom to do what we are most drawn to do, we usually do what we are best at. That usually makes us the best in the world in many ways. Even if you love to drive a car crazy fast and only know how to turn left, you can still make millions of dollars and be called a champion in America. The same can be said for a multitude of other professions and industries with so much greatness, well attended by an American presence.

It must be intimidating for the enemies of America that we are good at so much. They know that if an all-volunteer force of American warriors is coming that it will be formidable. Our civilian sector sets the standard for that and is actually the America we fight to defend. We love you, and we know that you maintain the country we defend.

Without greatness at home, no one would volunteer to fight for her. This should compel all of us to do our best each day. If you contribute to education, maintenance, production, sales, or in any way contribute to the landscape of America the Beautiful, then we veterans salute you. I also appreciate the ammunition and food that your tax dollars provided us in the field and around the world! If you've paid taxes, then you're a direct supporter of your warriors and a provider of decisive advantages on the battlefield.

But I've got a bone to pick with you. Stop acting like veterans are victims. Stop feeling sorry for veterans. Stop assuming that every veteran has PTSD, or that they are automatically rendered somehow impaired by it. Do not accept such a mindset from an American veteran, either. If you can't look to your war veterans for strength and leadership, then where can you look? Just because you didn't serve does not mean you can't have an opinion about it. Thank God the military doesn't lead itself. It is the American people through their government who determine the role of the military. Don't be afraid to tell us what you expect of us, both while in service and after we return home. I believe that you don't have to be there to understand. I believe that America has rebounded since the Vietnam era and become an immeasurably grateful nation for its troops. I believe that unless a veteran was serving him or herself, they owe the benefits of that experience to the country they were serving.

We are one team, and it is one fight. If you enjoy your own A-Team today, within your American life, then celebrate it! If you don't yet have that, then begin creating it for yourself.

Go, then. Build your A-Team!

ABOUT THE AUTHORS

Sgt. 1st Class Gregory A. Stube (Ret.)

Sgt. 1st Class Gregory A. Stube (Ret.) is from Covington, Tennessee. He spent nineteen of his twenty-three years in the U.S. Army serving as a Green Beret on the Special Forces' A-Teams. He was very seriously wounded during Operation Medusa in Afghanistan, September 2006. He spent a year recovering from his wounds in a hospital and went on to be the first spokesperson for the Green Berets. In addition to his service on the functional elements of the Green Berets, known as the A-team, Stube served as a trainer for the Special Forces Advanced Urban Combat Course and spent four years as cadre in the distinguished John F. Kennedy Special Warfare Center and School.

Stube joined the Army in 1988 as an infantryman. His awards include the Bronze Star, Purple Heart, multiple Army Commendation Medals, multiple Army Achievement Medals, the Good Conduct Medal, the National Defense Service Medal, the German Silver Marksmanship Award, as well as the Special Forces Tab and many other notable military honors.

Today, Stube joins us in the midst of his newest mission in life—his post-retirement objective of bringing home the leadership principles and values that he learned on the battlefield and in the hospital. He is now a well-known public speaker. His focus has been on leadership, character development, and helping other veterans become all they can be in civilian life.

Frank Miniter

Frank Miniter is the author of *Kill Big Brother*, a novel that shows how we can keep our freedom in this digital age. He is also the author of *The Ultimate Man's Survival Guide: Recovering the Lost Art of Manhood*, a

New York Times bestseller, and *This Will Make a Man of You—One Man's Search for Hemingway and Manhood in a Changing World*. Miniter is a contributor with *Forbes* and many other publications, and is a constant commentator on national radio and television shows.